About the author:

Richard J. Lowry (Ph.D., Brandeis University) is Associate Professor of Psychology at Vassar College. He is the editor of THE JOURNALS OF A. H. MASLOW (Brooks/Cole, 1973) and DOMINANCE, SELF-ESTEEM, SELF-ACTUALIZATION: GERMINAL PAPERS OF A. H. MASLOW (Brooks/Cole, 1973).

The A. H. Maslow Series

A. H. Maslow: An Intellectual Portrait
by Richard J. Lowry

The Journals of A. H. Maslow
by the late A. H. Maslow and edited by Richard J. Lowry

Dominance, Self-Esteem, Self-Actualization:
Germinal Papers of A. H. Maslow
by the late A. H. Maslow and edited by Richard J. Lowry

Abraham H. Maslow: A Memorial Volume

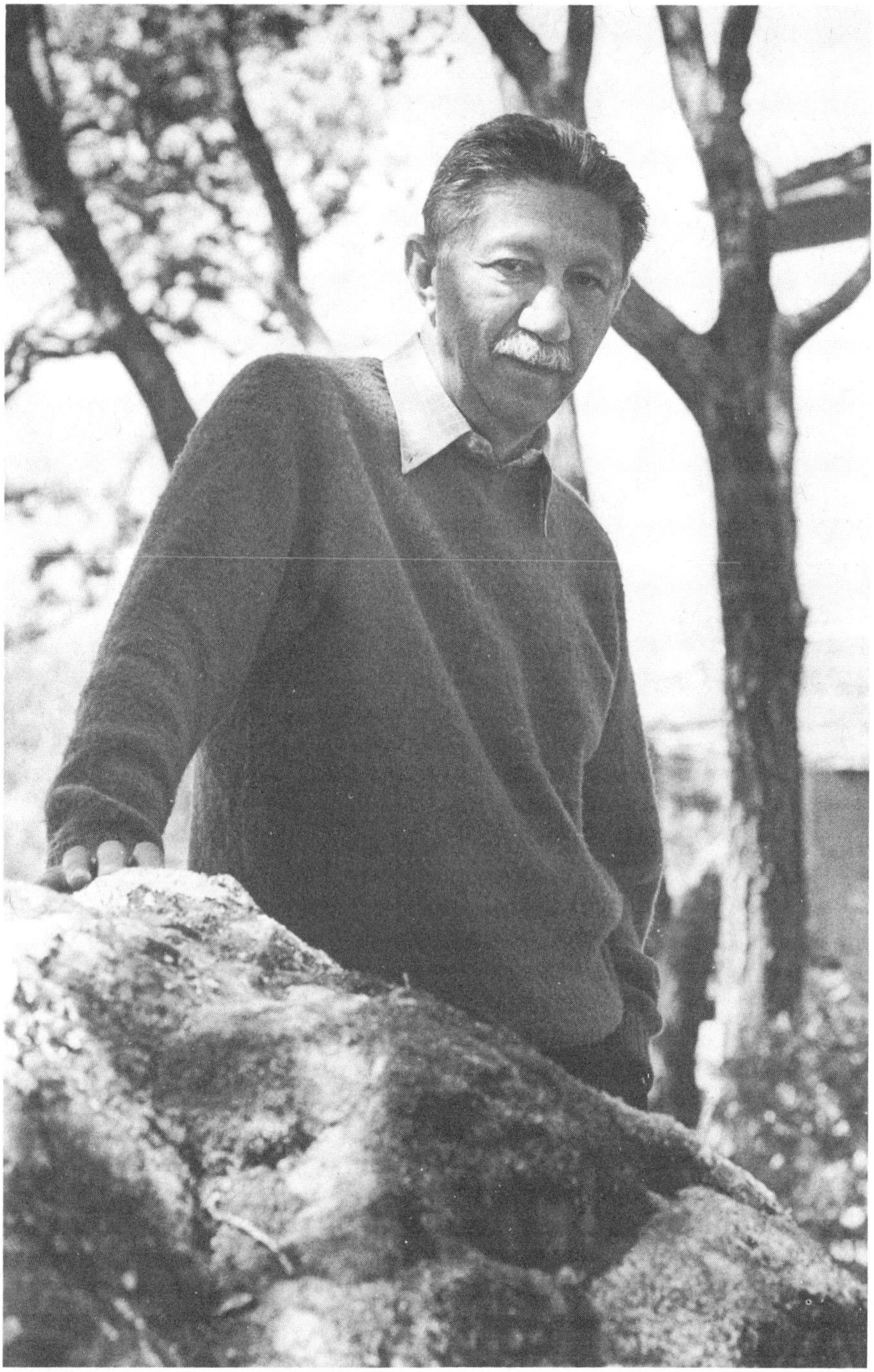

A. H. Maslow:
An Intellectual Portrait

Written for
The International Study Project, Inc.

by
Richard J. Lowry
Vassar College

Brooks/Cole Publishing Company
Monterey, California
A Division of Wadsworth Publishing Company, Inc.

Credits

Frontispiece photo by William Carter.

A. H. Maslow. Eupsychia—the good society. *Journal of Humanistic Psychology,* 1961, **1,** 1-11. Reprinted by permission.

A. H. Maslow. Psychological data and human values. In *New Knowledge in Human Values,* by A. H. Maslow. Copyright © 1959 by Harper & Row, Publishers, Inc. Reprinted by permission of the publishers.

A. H. Maslow. Cognition of being in the peak-experience. *Journal of Genetic Psychology,* 1959, **94,** 43-66. Copyright 1959 by the Journal Press. Reprinted by permission.

The Psychology of Science: A Reconnaissance, by A. H. Maslow. Copyright © 1966 by Harper & Row, Publishers, Inc. Reprinted by permission of the publishers.

A. H. Maslow. A theory of human motivation. *Psychological Review,* 1943, **50,** 370-396. Copyright 1943 by the American Psychological Association and reproduced by permission.

A. H. Maslow. Religions, values, and peak-experiences. Kappa Delta Pi Lecture Series. Copyright 1964 by Kappa Delta Pi. Reprinted by permission of Kappa Delta Pi, an Honor Society in Education.

ISBN: 0-8185-0083-2
L.C. Catalog Card No: 72-95177
Printed in the United States of America
1 2 3 4 5 6 7 8 9 10—77 76 75 74 73

This book was edited by Micky Lawler and designed by Linda Marcetti. It was typeset by Datagraphics, Inc., Phoenix, Arizona, and printed and bound by Kingsport Press, Kingsport, Tennessee.

To Jeannie and Heather

Interviewer: "Aren't these principles the same basic values that every religion and philosophy has attempted to find—a quest as old as cultures themselves? How does your approach as a psychologist differ from the philosopher or theologian?"

Maslow: "I think my approach differs tremendously. . . . It is certainly true that mankind, throughout history, has looked for guiding values, for principles of right and wrong. But he has tended to look outside of himself, outside of mankind, to a God, to some sort of sacred book perhaps, or to a ruling class. What I am doing is exploring the theory that you can find the values by which mankind must live, and for which man has always sought, by digging into the best people in depth. I believe, in other words, that I can find ultimate values which are right for mankind by observing the best of mankind. If, under the best conditions and in the best specimens, I simply stand aside and describe in a scientific way what these human values are, I find values that are the old values of truth, goodness, and beauty, and some additional ones as well—for instance, gaiety, justice, and joy."—Radio Interview, 1960.

Preface

Any attempt to portray the concrete workings of a person's mind must fall somewhat short of the mark. This one falls even shorter—partly because the mind that it seeks to portray was so rich and complex and partly because the book had to be kept as concise as possible. I am satisfied that it is a good book as far as it goes and that it can be read with profit by anyone interested in Maslow and his work. But I must urge the reader to bear in mind that, although A. H. Maslow was *at least* the man I have described herein, he was also more—far more. This book purports to paint his "intellectual portrait," but all it really does is sketch the bare outlines.

Another point I must make is that, although this book is a work of fondness and respect for Maslow, it is not a labor of discipleship. It should go without saying that I consider his approach to psychology to contain a great deal of value. But though I have tried to keep my own predilections under steady reign, the reader will still discern readily enough that I would part company with Maslow at many turns. These predilections have undoubtedly colored my treatment throughout; I can only hope that they have not done so to the point of distortion. At any rate, my attempt has been to strike a proper balance between sympathetic understanding on the one hand and critical skepticism on the other. I am sure that this is the way Maslow himself would have wanted it.

There is one person without whom, truly, this book could not have been written. It is Mrs. Bertha Maslow, who first aroused my interest in the undertaking, who then helped to arrange for its material support, and who finally served throughout as patient soundingboard and invaluable source of information and ideas. Mrs. Maslow has told me on several occasions that she is "not an intellectual." I think she is too modest, for she has never failed to exhibit to me one of the finest and most essential characteristics of the true intellectual: a devotion to the plain, unvarnished truth of things. At no time did she encourage me to build a pious monument to her late husband; her only admonition was "Be sure that it is a sound, critical, scholarly job."

I am also very much indebted to Vassar College, which provided me with a year's leave during which I was able to work on this and other matters pertaining to Maslow; to Ricardo B. Morant of Brandeis University, who was kind enough to read and comment on the entire book in manuscript; and to everyone associated with the International Study Project, Inc., of Menlo Park, California, which provided material support for the project—especially William Price Laughlin, William Crockett, and Mrs. Kay Pontius.

I cannot close this preface, or begin the book, without a brief personal recollection. I first met Maslow in early 1962, during my first year of graduate study in psychology. He had just returned from a semester's leave, and I, eager to meet the Great Man of the department, descended upon him almost the moment he walked through the door. I do not remember much of our initial conversation, but I do recall one thing that has stayed with me ever since. At one point the talk turned to the question of what one must do in order to be a good psychologist. Maslow's answer was unequivocal: first, you must love psychology with a passion; second, you must put in at least eighty hours of good hard work each week. Well, I cannot say that I have put in my eighty hours each and every week since then; and there have been times when it seemed to me a mystery how anyone could love psychology except its mother. But since that time I have never doubted, even for a moment, that that is what a good psychologist *is*. I have also never doubted that Maslow *was* one.

Richard J. Lowry

Contents

A. H. Maslow:
An Intellectual Portrait

1

Ideals and Over-Beliefs

> The most interesting and valuable things about a man are his ideals and over-beliefs. The same is true of nations and historic epochs; and the excesses of which the particular individuals and epochs are guilty are compensated in the total, and become profitable to mankind in the long run.—William James, Preface to *The Will to Believe and Other Essays in Popular Philosophy* (1897).

Some men pass their entire lives without ever having anything that might be called an intellectual awakening. A. H. Maslow was not one of these. Neither was he a man whose intellectual awakening came gradually and imperceptibly. For him it came, as it were, in a flash.

It happened in 1927, when he was nineteen years old and a sophomore at the City College of New York. Some thirty-five years later he wrote of the experience as follows:

> I registered for a course in the Philosophy of Civilization that was too difficult for me. I finally dropped out, to the poorly concealed contempt of my professor. And yet this turned out to be one of the most important educational experiences of my life, because it introduced me to William Graham Sumner's *Folkways,* which changed my life. But this is exactly what our professor warned us about in his first lecture of the semester. "If you really read this book you can never be the same again. You can never again be an innocent." He was right.[1]

Maslow went on to say that what Sumner's book did for him was to disabuse him of his "simple, unquestioning ethnocentrism" and of the tacit supposi-

[1]Unpublished notes, 1962.

tion that his society was the "fixed truth from which everything else was a foolish falling away." It doubtless did all this, but it did something else as well: it introduced him to a *theoria,* a point of view, a way of seeing things.

Though Sumner's *Folkways* mentioned Darwin only once, and evolution not at all, it was in fact a sustained attempt to apply the broader implications of Darwinian evolutionary doctrine to the forms and norms of human society. The principal argument of the book was that the mores or "folkways" of human societies *evolve*—in accordance with basic biological needs and environmental contingencies and as a result of something akin to the Darwinian process of natural selection. There was then a corollary thesis, sometimes spoken of as the principle of cultural relativity: although the biological exigencies may be the same for all men and for all societies, the nature and pattern of environmental contingencies will differ from one society to another; accordingly, different societies will evolve different ways—different mores or folkways—for meeting the same basic biological exigencies. Finally, there was an evaluative component to the argument: the differing folkways of various societies are to be judged only by the efficiency and expedience with which they meet and satisfy biological exigency; in and of themselves they are neither good nor bad, superior nor inferior. The argument is best summarized in Sumner's own words:

> Every moment [in life] brings necessities which must be satisfied at once. Need [is therefore] the first experience [of primitive men and primitive society], and it [is] followed at once by a blundering effort to satisfy it. . . . The method is that of trial and failure, which produces repeated pain, loss, and disappointments. Nevertheless, it is a method of rude experiment and selection. The earliest efforts of men were of this kind. Need was the impelling force. Pleasure and pain . . . were the rude constraints which defined the line on which efforts must proceed. . . . Thus ways of doing things were selected which were expedient. They answered the purpose better than other ways, or with less toil and pain. Along the course on which efforts were compelled to go, habit, routine, and skill were developed. The struggle to maintain existence was carried on, not individually, but in groups. Each profited by the other's experience; hence there was concurrence towards that which proved to be most expedient. . . . In this way folkways arise.[2]

It is easy in retrospect to see the enduring effects that Sumner's *Folkways* was to have on Maslow's intellectual development. First there was the notion of basic human needs, of inborn biological necessity, which was later to be reflected in Maslow's conception of "instinctoid" human nature. (The idea of basic human needs was hardly unique with Sumner, but its statement in *Folkways* does seem to have been Maslow's earliest acquaintance with it.) Then, too, Maslow surely must have found in Sumner's book a foreshadowing of Ruth Benedict's conception of "synergy," which he was to

[2]W. G. Sumner, *Folkways* (New York: New American Library, 1960), p. 18.

make so much of in later years. (Sumner had written at some length on the "consistency" of folkways.) Finally, and perhaps most importantly, there was what Maslow's unnamed professor warned him about when he said "You can never again be an innocent." It is doubtful that Maslow or anyone else could lose every last shred and vestige of "simple, unquestioning ethnocentrism." Nevertheless, from that movement on, Maslow's reflections on human nature and human society were to be tempered perforce by cross-cultural considerations.

He was, indeed, quite "smitten with anthropology" ever after. He had read Sumner in 1927. In 1928 he transferred to the University of Wisconsin, and there he went on to devour the works of Margaret Mead, Branislaw Malinowski, and Ruth Benedict. Ralph Linton, then a professor at Wisconsin, was his wife's teacher and "*sort of* a friend" of his. "I got so fired up with anthropology," Maslow recalled some forty years later,

> that I gave lectures on various aspects of what today we would call culture and personality, in W. H. Sheldon's psychology classes, in Harry Harlow's introductory psychology course, and in one other. . . . During these graduate years I wrote a chapter on culture and personality for Ross Stagner's *Psychology of Personality* text. I do believe that this was the first one written by any psychologist. . . . When I came to New York in 1935, I sat in on as many anthropology classes and seminars as I could with Ruth Benedict, Alexander Lesser, George Herzog, and lectured to the anthropology club. I was a member of the American Anthropological Association and gave papers at the conventions.[3]

In the late 1930s Maslow even spent an anthropological summer among the Northern Blackfoot Indians near Calgary—an experience to which he was to refer time and again in later years. He went into the summer with sincere hopes of keeping "in touch with other cultures through the rest of my life." He came out of it with the discovery that he was "too much a family man. I very much missed my wife and new baby, and I didn't dare take them to the Blackfoot for fear of trachoma and TB."

In any event, let it be noted that Maslow's intellectual awakening came, by his own reckoning, in 1927 with his discovery of Sumner's *Folkways*. And then, only a year or so later, he had what amounted to a second intellectual awakening: he was introduced to psychology by way of John B. Watson's "beautiful program" of behaviorism. Actually, records concerning Maslow's discovery of psychology are curiously lacking. We do know that he had a course in introductory psychology at the City College of New York in the fall semester of 1927 (the same semester in which he read Sumner's *Folkways*). In the diaries that he kept for that year he noted that he had the course, that he at one point had a long talk with the professor and received from him a

[3]Unpublished letter, 1967.

list of books to read, and that he received a grade of C in the course. Nowhere, however, did he reflect on the subject matter of the course or exhibit any enthusiasm for it. In the spring semester of that same academic year, 1927-1928, he transferred to Cornell, where he had a course in "Elementary Psychology" with the famous E. B. Titchener—though there is no record of his having been inspired by Titchener's brand of psychology either.

At the beginning of the next academic year, 1928-1929, Maslow transferred to the University of Wisconsin. The department of psychology at Wisconsin in the late 1920s and early 1930s was a virtual galaxy of psychological stars—Norman Cameron, Harry Harlow, Clark L. Hull, Richard W. Husband, Arthur Jersild, and William H. Sheldon, to mention only some. It was also something of a hotbed for the comparatively new psychological doctrine of behaviorism, which seemed to many psychologists at the time to be the wave of the future. Maslow did not come to Wisconsin seeking psychology, but there he seems to have found it nonetheless. And there he remained through the completion of his A. B. (1930) and Ph.D. (1934) and then for another year (1934-1935) as a Teaching Fellow in psychology.

In later years Maslow was to recount that his first enthusiasm for psychology was inspired by Watson's behaviorism, especially by its technological promise and utopian vision. It is perhaps difficult for the psychology student of today to appreciate just how much enthusiasm Watson's behavioristic vision did inspire among bright young persons in the 1920s and 1930s. Nowadays Watson's behaviorism is usually seen as simply an early and rather naïve attempt to turn psychology into a genuine experimental science. It was of course this, but it was much else besides; for Watson sought nothing less than to provide a definitive doctrine of human nature, an "experimental ethic," and "*a foundation for all* future experimental ethics." The following passage, taken from the closing page of his *Behaviorism* of 1924, expresses a theme that was woven through the whole fabric of his work:

> I think behaviorism [lays] a foundation for saner living. . . . I wish I had time more fully to describe this, to picture to you the kind of rich and wonderful individual we should make of every healthy child if only we could let it shape itself properly and then provide for it a universe in which it could exercise that organization—a universe unshackled by legendary folk lore of happenings thousands of years ago [he was of course alluding here to religion]; unhampered by disgraceful political history; free of foolish customs and conventions which have no significance in themselves [cf. Sumner's *Folkways*], yet which hem the individual in like taut steel bands. . . . For the universe will change if you bring up your children, not in the freedom of the libertine, but in behavioristic freedom—a freedom which we cannot even picture in words, so little do we know of it.[4]

Watson never did get around to picturing his "behavioristic freedom" in words, but that did not seem to matter at the time. What did matter was that

[4]J. B. Watson, *Behaviorism* (New York: Norton, 1924), pp. 247–248.

here was a vision—secular and ostensibly scientific—of a better world, indeed, a perfect world. It was a vision that could scarcely help appealing to
a young man who was to record, some forty years later, that the whole of his
work had been determined by his "Jewish passion for ethics, utopianism,
Messianism, the prophetic thundering." Maslow's "Jewish passion" was of
course thoroughly secularized, and so it had no difficulty consorting with
behaviorism, even though the latter was, and remains, a kind of secularized
version of the Protestant Ethic. Strange bedfellows, Maslow and Watson?
Perhaps. But let us remember that Watson, at the time, had the only bed in
town.

All of this notwithstanding, Maslow seems to have begun sliding out
of Watson's bed fairly soon after he climbed in. Beginning apparently in his
early years of graduate study, he grew progressively disaffected with behaviorism—not so much with its utopian vision as with the narrowness of the
lenses through which the vision was seen. The following journal entry of
August 1968 is probably an accurate résumé of his defection:

> Behaviorism has done a lot. It was the beautiful program of Watson that
> brought me into psychology. But its fatal flaw is that it's good for the lab
> and in the lab, but you put it on and take it off like a lab coat. It's useless
> at home with your kids and wife and friends. It does not generate an [ade-
> quate] image of man, a philosophy of life, a conception of human nature. It's
> not [an adequate] guide to living, to values, to choices. . . . If you try to treat
> your children at home in the same way you treat your animals in the lab,
> your wife will scratch your eyes out. (My wife ferociously warned me against
> experimenting on her babies; I was working with monkeys at the time.)

And so he did not stay long with behaviorism. But he did stay long enough
to be "smitten" by psychology, to complete a Ph.D. in psychology, and to
become what he was to be, with a passion, for the rest of his life: a psychologist.

The Young Psychologist

In his last undergraduate year at Wisconsin (1929–1930), Maslow
became research assistant to William H. Sheldon, who was later to be known
for his studies of the relationship between "somatotype" and personality. He
remained with Sheldon for a while but at length began to "consider the work
unfruitful and after a private conversation with Professor Clark L. Hull
dropped [it] and began to prepare myself in experimental psychology."

It was under this latter enthusiasm that he went on to do his master's
thesis, which was as orthodox an example of "experimental psychology" as
one could ever hope to find: "The Effect of Varying External Conditions on

Learning, Retention and Reproduction."[5] He continued on this same unexceptional path until 1931–1932, when, as he recorded, "my interests definitely turned to primate psychology," where they remained for the next several years. The first fruit of his interest in primate psychology was an experimental study of "delayed reaction" in primates, published in 1932 and carried out under the direction of Harry F. Harlow.[6] After this study was completed, he then went on his own initiative to New York, where he conducted a similar study on the primates in the Bronx Zoo.

Shortly thereafter, again on his own initiative, Maslow undertook a study of the food preferences of primates.[7] This was perhaps his first psychological study that was distinctly his own. Its results indicated that there is far greater variability in the food preferences of primates than in those, say, of the rat. In this respect—variability of food preferences—primate animals were seen to be much closer to man than were rats, and yet it was on the study of hungry rats that most of the experimental psychology of motivation had been based. Maslow went on to argue that this was not only a mistake but a fundamental mistake. In dealing with hungry rats, we need hardly be concerned with individual differences in food preference, for these differences are so slight as to be negligible. In dealing with hungry primates and humans, however, we must be very much concerned indeed with individual food preferences. The argument, of course, applies not just to hunger but to other motivational states as well. Its broader implication was simply that, if we are to study lower animals in the hope of learning something about man, we would do well to begin with those lower animals, the primates, that are most closely related to man.

The highpoint of Maslow's interest in primate psychology was marked by his studies of primate dominance and submission, which began with his doctoral dissertation of 1934.[8] These were the studies with which he first made a name for himself in psychology. Not only were they intelligently conceived and executed, but they were as fine an example of psychological observation as is to be found anywhere. It is difficult to read Maslow's descriptions of primate dominant-submissive relationships without seeing in them a kind of parody of human social relationships. Thus, Maslow found,

[5]A. H. Maslow, "The Effect of Varying External Conditions on Learning, Retention and Reproduction." *Journal of Experimental Psychology*, 1934, **17**, 36–47.

[6]A. H. Maslow, "Delayed Reaction Tests on Primates from the Lemur to the Orangoutan" (with Harry Harlow and Harold Uehling). *Journal of Comparative Psychology*, 1932, **13**, 313–343.

[7]A. H. Maslow, "Food Preferences of Primates." *Journal of Comparative Psychology*, 1933, **16**, 187–197; and "Appetites and Hungers in Animal Motivation." 1935, **20**, 75–83.

[8]A. H. Maslow, "The Role of Dominance in the Social and Sexual Behavior of Infra-Human Primates: I. Observations at Vilas Park Zoo." *Journal of Genetic Psychology*, 1936, **48**, 261–277; "II. An Experimental Determination of the Dominance Behavior Syndrome." 1936, **48**, 278–309; "III. A Theory of Sexual Behavior of Infra-Human Primates." 1936, **48**, 310–338; "IV. The Determination of Hierarchy in Pairs and Groups." 1936, **49**, 161–198.

if any two primates of the same species are put together, one will come to be dominant, the other submissive. The dominant member of the pair will then have the following prerogatives and responsibilities: (1) it will tend to preempt all or most of a limited food supply; (2) it will frequently mount the submissive member in the mating posture, irrespective of the sex of the two animals (the submissive member, on the other hand, will characteristically present itself for mounting as a sign of submissiveness); (3) the dominant member will frequently bully the submissive member but is almost never bullied by it; (4) the dominant member initiates most of the fighting that occurs in the pair, and it never cringes under aggression from the subordinate member (although it may at times permit itself a strategic retreat); (5) the dominant member is in general more active than the submissive one; thus, it is likely to do more grooming than the submissive animal, to initiate more play, and so on. Maslow then went on to observe that primate dominance relationships grow much more complex as the size of the group increases. For as the primate group increases in size, complex alliances are entered into, and so we must speak not of simple dominance relationships but of dominance hierarchies. He also suggested that primate sexual behavior may sometimes be motivated as much by the dominance drive as by the physiological sex drive, and he attempted on this basis to explain a number of primate sexual behaviors such as homosexuality, sadomasochism, and freedom from sexual cyclicity. He also pointed out the similarity between his concept of "dominance" and Alfred Adler's notion of "masculine protest."

These primate dominance studies were of course fraught with implications for human psychology as well, and indeed a few years afterward Maslow did undertake to study dominance and submission at the human level.[9] These human researches soon led him in another direction, however, so we shall postpone them until a later chapter.

Maslow first reported on his primate dominance research at the 1935 convention of the American Psychological Association. As it happened, the chairman of the paper session at which he presented his report was the great Edward L. Thorndike, who had been well known within American psychology for the better part of three decades. Although Thorndike disagreed with some of Maslow's conclusions, he was nonetheless impressed with the research and with the young psychologist who had produced it. And so he invited Maslow to come to Columbia University with him and work as his research associate. Maslow happily accepted the invitation and spent the next two academic years as a Carnegie Fellow at Columbia.

One of the projects on which Maslow worked with Thorndike was described as "a study (in part) of the instincts which any economic or political order *must* take into account in dealing with the individuals which constitute

[9]A. H. Maslow, "Dominance-Feeling, Personality, and Social Behavior in Women." *Journal of Social Psychology*, 1939, **10**, 3–39.

it, if such an order is to avoid trouble and is to perpetuate itself." Maslow's first task in this project seems to have been to write, solely for Thorndike's inspection, a brief statement of his own views on "the instinct problem." This statement is especially interesting, since it fairly well summarizes the views that Maslow had at the time on the psychology of motivation. Its central message was conveyed by the charming phrase "Certain drives there are, and satisfied they will be in one way or another." The syntax was perhaps more Yiddish than English, but the meaning was plain enough: "Human nature is *not* indefinitely malleable." To be sure, its manifestation may be largely determined by the "governmental, economic, and social taboos extant at the time." But throughout all such affectations there remains a basic, virtually unmodifiable "core" of human need, drive, and motive. There is, in short, an "intrinsic human nature"; and the task of psychology is to discover what that nature is. At the time this statement was written, Maslow was still convinced that "the phylogenetic approach" was the most promising, the most "beautiful method for a determination of [what] that intrinsic human nature may be."

Maslow left Thorndike and Columbia in 1937, having accepted a teaching appointment at Brooklyn College. He remained, however, in New York City, which in the late 1930s was a very exciting place indeed for a young psychologist to be. In Maslow's case it was all the more so, for it was here that he came into contact with some of the greatest names in American and European psychology and anthropology—Max Wertheimer, Kurt Koffka, Alfred Adler, Karen Horney, Ruth Benedict, Margaret Mead, Gregory Bateson, and Alexander Lesser, to mention but a few. It was during this time that Maslow became intimately acquainted with those two fairly new imports from Europe, psychoanalysis and the psychology of Gestalt.

Something else important was also happening in the late 1930s. It was becoming increasingly evident—painfully evident—that the world would soon be at war. Of course, any sensitive and intelligent man would be disturbed by the prospect of an approaching world war, but for Maslow there seems to have been more at stake. War, when it came, would surely be with Germany. The Nazi party had come to power in Germany in the early 1930s (at about the same time that Maslow was beginning his studies of primate dominance), and since that time it had become increasingly clear that one of the principal thrusts of the Nazi movement was an unblushing anti-Semitic crusade. Already, by the late 1930s, the Jews of Germany had been deprived of their German citizenship, and their lives and properties were insecure to say the least. Moreover, it was becoming every day more obvious that the Nazi program included the intention of making Germany, and perhaps the whole of Europe, *Judenrein*. Now Maslow was a Jew, but only by an accident of birth. He was a Jew, but a nonreligious, emancipated, and thoroughly secularized Jew. Or so, at least, he had formerly thought. But now, in the New

York City of the late 1930s, he was confronted on every side with refugee German Jews, equally emancipated and secularized but the victims of anti-Semitic persecution nonetheless. And for every German Jew who had come to New York as a refugee, he knew that there were hundreds and thousands still in Germany who had not been so fortunate. In brief, the same thing happened to Maslow as happened to a great many other emancipated and secularized American Jews in the late 1930s. And so it was that he was much more keenly disturbed by the approaching cataclysm than were most of his fellow American psychologists.

In any case, the ever-darkening hue of world events in those days profoundly affected him and eventually caused the course of his life to take a major turning. Up until this time he had accepted and abided by the principle that psychology should seek after its portion of truth patiently, slowly, cautiously, one small step after the other. Now, on the contrary, he was beginning to feel that the world needed psychology's portion of truth not in the indefinite future but *now!* And so it was, around this time, that he began to be possessed by a sense of urgency. It was then, too, that his research interests turned from the rigorous fields of experimental comparative psychology to the more treacherous but—as he was beginning to think—richer soil of social psychology, abnormal psychology, and the psychology of human personality and motivation. In 1937 he began publishing his studies of human "dominance-feeling," later called "self-esteem." In 1941 appeared his classic *Principles of Abnormal Psychology* (with Bela Mittelmann). In 1942 he published such titles as "Liberal Leadership and Personality" and "A Comparative Approach to the Problem of Destructiveness," and in 1943 appeared his well-known "Theory of Human Motivation." This, then, is the path that Maslow took in the late 1930s and the one on which he remained, venturing ever farther along it, for the rest of his years.

Although this turning point in Maslow's life was caused largely by his disturbance over the darkness of world events, there was probably something else at work too. Up until this time Maslow had always been, in one way or another, a subordinate. He had been a student for six years at the University of Wisconsin; then, even after completing his Ph.D., he stayed on for another year in a junior capacity. Following his seven years at Wisconsin, he worked as a junior research associate with Thorndike for another two years. Finally, in 1937, he went out on his own; and that, coincidentally, is when the turning began. Many indeed are the young psychologists—it is doubtless true in other fields as well—who thrive and flourish as long as they are someone's student or research associate but who, when finally they venture out on their own, simply languish and fade away into obscurity. The phenomenon probably has something to do with what Riesman has spoken of as "inner-directedness." If a man has inner-direction, he will, when on his own, find it and follow it. If he does not have it, he will more likely persist on the path that he followed as a subordinate, his pace getting slower year by year until at last he stops. Maslow had his full share of inner-direction, and now that he was his own man, he was beginning to follow it. But to understand just what form this inner-direction took, we shall have to go back about a decade and then return by way of a rather tortuous trail.

"Wonderful Possibilities, Inscrutable Depths"

Among the many unpublished writings of Maslow's that have survived is a handwritten undergraduate philosophy paper entitled "The Over-Soul—Emerson" and dated October 23, 1928, which was about a year after his discovery of Sumner's *Folkways*. Considered simply as a work of undergraduate scholarship, it is an entirely undistinguished production. The grade that the young Maslow received on it is not known, but it was probably not a very high one. Nonetheless, the paper is as remarkable and revealing a document as the historian or biographer might ever hope to find. It expresses something of the essence of Maslow's mind and character, and so we present it here in its entirety (except for its closing paragraph, to which we shall return in a moment).

The Over-Soul—Emerson
A. H. Maslow
October 23, 1928

I abhor, with all the vehemence that is in me, Emerson and his like. I have an illustrious excuse and example. Schopenhauer inveighed with all the might of his piercing satire against those whom he called "metaphysicians of the people," and I am sure he would have included among these Emerson.

Let us lay down our reasons in hard words. Emerson, I say, is a wordy preacher, a superstitious mystic, a shoddy thinker (if I can dignify him by even calling him thinker), and finally as bad a philosopher as it is possible for a man to be. He rises calmly above all logic and rules of thought by which all other poor mortals are constrained. He is but a poet (a poor one to be sure) masquerading as a deep thinker.

First of all and most important, Emerson believes or believed in a personal God, a resurrection, and all the other paraphernalia and stock in trade of the New England minister. This automatically debars him from being placed in the ranks of philosophy, which is a denial of all dogma, revelation, and supernaturalism. Theology attempts to find its justification outside itself, but philosophy has no authorities to appeal to and no absolute criteria to measure its concepts by. I am willing, then, to admit Emerson as a theologian, but as a philosopher—never!

To kill every last vestige of any claims he may lay to being one, it is necessary only to analyze a few of his sentences at random. I call them sentences in the judicial sense of the term, for Emerson judges the universe with a cool self-assurance and confidence that are hardly justified by the facts. Let us analyze his thoughts, for instance, just as they come, beginning with the first page.

He begins at once by saying that there are some moments whose depth leads us to ascribe to them more reality than we do to others. He looks back here to Descartes, who said that things are most real when they are most distinct, a very poor criterion of reality indeed, on the face of it.

Then he goes on to say that the universal sense of something lacking, something wanting, establishes a higher origin for events than the human will. "We grant that human life is mean; but how did we find out it was mean?" As much as to say that by finding fault with something, we tacitly compare it with an ideal. And when we do compare anything with an ideal, then the ideal exists. This again I pass over with no comment. It is so ridiculously absurd that it calls down ridicule on itself.

These ideas I infer of course. Emerson hides his few weak ideas under a tremendously rushing torrent of words, words, words that overcome us and carry us along dazed on the crest of its wave. Getting at his ideas is like peeling an onion. We take off the first coat and the second, and then the third and so on. When we have taken off all the coats, there is nothing left.

Then he goes on to propound his doctrine of the Over-Soul. Here again, he is so vague and his language so flowery that again we cannot set forth a clear-cut, consistent, plausible doctrine. At one second, he seems to deny all reality, somewhat as Schopenhauer did, ascribing reality only to the Platonic Ideas (which in Emerson is the Over-Soul). Perhaps this is what Emerson meant; perhaps it is not. I, for the life of me, can't tell. What *can* a man mean by saying "that great nature in which we rest, as the earth lies in the soft arms of the atmosphere"?

At one moment he gives us the impression that this Over-Soul is *in* man himself. He calls it "that common heart." Again he says "within man is the soul of the whole." He even goes on to include good-heartedly and gener-ously the sun, the moon, the animal, the tree. Is this hylozoism? Or perhaps pantheism? At another place, a half-page further, he turns squarely and gives us the impression that this Over-Soul is *outside* of man, governing and controlling him, like a personal God.

What shall we say to all this confusion, these muddling sentences, these conflicting ideas? How shall we regard this man who faces in all directions at once as well as up and down? But he doesn't stop there. He subscribes to pantheism, hylozoism, and mysticism. All in the short space of two pages of writing. Is this philosophy? It is not. What is it? It is rhetorical stupidity! It is bosh!

Need I go on to show how his conception of the soul as a little mannequin within us is just as stupid a doctrine? Must I refute his statement that "The blindness of the intellect begins when it would be something of itself!"? Instances multiply endlessly.

I had intended to spend some time on pointing out the lack of plan, of form, the lack of a single underlying thought in the rest of the essay, but an analysis of three pages has given us as much as we need and more.

I pass over too the errors into which his rhetoric consistently lead him, and the myriad meanings with which he invests his every word in accordance with what he wants to say. It is unnecessary, I think, to go into these, for

I think I can rest my case on the very few examples I have herein set forth.
. . .

Maslow's paper had a certain raw *chutzpah* about it that was bound
to rough the nerves of any man worth his professorial salt. Nonetheless, the
comments that the professor in the course, Max Otto, appended to the paper
were a model of pedagogical restraint. "You write with vigor," he observed,

> and there is something appealing about that. At the same time, I cannot say
> much for your air of finality when you allow yourself to make quite un-
> founded statements. Take your accusation that Emerson believed in a per-
> sonal God, the resurrection, and all the other stock in trade of the New
> England minister. Can you possibly back that up? . . . [Further examples of
> the same sort are then given.] Why go on with your paper? I hope you can
> keep the directness and force of your criticism and associate it with more
> accurate knowledge.

Although Professor Otto could not have known it at the time, he was
putting his finger on stylistic tendencies that were to remain with his young
student in greater or lesser degree throughout his life. It is certainly true that
almost everything Maslow wrote he wrote with "vigor." It is also true that
his writings, at least his later ones, retained a certain "air of finality" and that
they were not often weighted down with the disciplinary conventions or
technical apparatus of pedantic scholarship. More important than the stylistic
tendencies revealed by the paper, however, are the tendencies of attitude and
belief. Recall the opening lines: "I abhor, with all the vehemence that is in
me, Emerson and his like. . . . Emerson, I say, is a wordy preacher, a superstitious mystic, a shoddy thinker (if I can dignify him by even calling him
thinker), and finally as bad a philosopher as it is possible for a man to be."
The "vehemence" continued throughout the paper. Whatever could have
possessed this normally shy Jewish boy from Brooklyn, newly arrived at the
University of Wisconsin, to inveigh so mightily? The plain truth of the matter
is that the author of this vituperative little paper had an ax to grind. He was
an atheist. More than that, he was a proud, militant atheist. Indeed, he was
at this time even something of a village atheist, avidly taking potshots at any
"wordy preacher" or "superstitious mystic" who came within range. And so
it was that he could confidently dismiss "Emerson and his like" after examining only three pages of the latter's writings: "Is this philosophy? It is not.
What is it? It is rhetorical stupidity! It is bosh!"

Of course, undergraduate atheism was not an unheard-of phenomenon in 1928, even at the University of Wisconsin. Maslow, however, did not
acquire his prized atheism as an undergraduate. On the contrary, he seems
to have been carrying it around with him for quite some time. In a tape-
recorded interview made toward the end of his life, Maslow recounted that
he had been a "scientist"—by which he meant tough-minded skeptic—

when I was four years old. I remember because my mother was very superstitious, and I mixed in religion with superstititon [she was also a very "religious person," at least as regards the outward observances of orthodox
Judaism], and I kept on testing her superstitions. You know, she would say
. . . "don't step over the leg of your brother, because he will stop growing
immediately." So what I did was to step over the legs of the brother. Then
she said . . . "you mustn't go through a window because you will go blind."
. . . Oh, she had lots of them. So I went through a window, and I remember
testing all these things at the age of four, five, and six.

The diaries that Maslow kept during his high school years show that, for a
variety of reasons, he had an intense disaffection for his "superstitious" and
"religious" mother even then. His father, whom he apparently respected and
identified with, was on the other hand an avowed freethinker. Add to all this
the general climate of the 1920s and 1930s—a climate that nurtured extremes
and contrarieties of all sorts—and you have the psychodynamic makings of
a militant young atheist.

It is perhaps worthwhile to note in passing that Sumner's views on
religion squared quite nicely with those of the young Maslow. (Sumner had
begun his career as an Episcopalian clergyman but abandoned the profession
long before writing *Folkways,* on the grounds that every moment spent on
metaphysics, philosophy, and theology is "worse than wasted.") Sumner
observed that, although folkways do indeed arise from practical, utilitarian
expedience, they arise in another way as well. For there was always an
element in human experience

> which was irrational and defied all expedient methods. One might use the
> best-known means with the greatest care, yet fail of the result. On the other
> hand, one might get a great result with no effort at all. One might also incur
> a calamity without any fault of his own. This was the aleatory element in
> life, the element of risk and loss, good or bad fortune.

It is precisely this aleatory element, Sumner held, that has "always been the
connecting link between the struggle for existence and religion." For it was
in seeking to control these uncontrollable chance occurrences that "primitive
men" first hit upon religious rites and beliefs. These, without exception,

> lacked all connection with facts, and were arbitrary constructions put upon
> experience. They were poetic and developed by poetic construction and
> imagination. The nexus between them and events was not cause and effect,
> but magic. They therefore led to delusive deductions in regard to life and its
> meaning, which entered into subsequent action as guiding faiths, and imper-
> ative notions about the conditions of success. [Thus] the authority of religion
> and that of custom coalesced into one indivisible obligation.[10]

[10]Sumner, *Folkways,* pp. 21–22.

One readily imagines the militant young atheist reading all this and vigorously nodding his head in agreement.

In any case, Maslow became a confirmed atheist early in his life and remained one throughout. Thus, even in his full maturity, we find him taking every opportunity to get in his licks at religious "superstition" and "supernaturalism." His public utterances on the subject were of course tempered by considerations of tact, but the opinions recorded in the privacy of his journals left no mistake about it: as far as Maslow could see, theistic religion was nothing but "crap" and a "childish looking for a Big Daddy in the sky." In this respect at least, he was the brother of the theist, albeit estranged: for theism and atheism are both, literally, superstitions—or, as William James put it, "over-beliefs." They are also forces that can guide a man's thought and conduct throughout his life.

Maslow was the brother of the theist in another respect as well. For though he was an atheist, he nonetheless had a keen sense of what Rudolf Otto has spoken of as *das Heilige*—the holy. And so, having gone to such length to acknowledge Maslow's atheism, we must now turn around to show that it was, even in his undergraduate days, an atheism of a very peculiar sort. Not the least part of the difference was this: Maslow, confirmed atheist though he was, had seen the face of God! Better said, he had known, or enjoyed, or suffered, an experience of the sort that generations of theists had *mistaken* for the face of God. Thus began the closing paragraph of his paper on Emerson:

> As for his proof of the existence of the Over-Soul by the mystic experience, I have but this to say. I have myself had the mystic experience . . . [in which] I experienced a blind groping for something, an overwhelming sense of unsatisfied desire, a helplessness which was so intense that it left me almost weeping.

As far as is known, this is the only mention that Maslow ever made of his youthful "mystic experience." We cannot know the circumstances that attended the experience; even less can we know the experience itself. But it clearly had a profound and lasting effect. In any case, by mentioning his experience in this paper, the young Maslow was seeking to make a point of criticism: Emerson's shoddy thinking notwithstanding, it is possible to have the mystic experience and yet to remain ideologically pure—that is, innocent of theistic superstitions. Thus, he virtuously hastened to aver, "I have myself had the mystic experience . . . and never did I ascribe it to any Over-Soul or any other such concept."

If Maslow's experience did not suggest to him an Over-Soul, a god, or something equally "superstitious," then just what did it portend? The answer that he gave, the last words in an otherwise undistinguished paper, partook of that ingenuous eloquence that was later to distinguish him. "At the moment of the mystic experience," he wrote,

we see wonderful possibilities and inscrutable depths in mankind. . . . Why
not ascribe [the wonder of the experience] to man himself? Instead of deducing from the mystic experience the essential helplessness and smallness of
man . . ., can we not round out a larger, more wonderful conception of the
greatness of the human species and the wonderful vistas of progress just
faintly glimpsed against the future?

The experience, then, reveals the hidden face not of God but of man! And
it is a far greater and more wonderful face than our normal, everyday experience might ever lead us to imagine. It is true that Maslow's sense of the holy
attached itself to man rather than to a "Big Daddy in the sky," but it was a
sense of the holy all the same.

The point to be made by all this is not simply that Maslow was a
"tough-minded" atheist or a "tender-minded" mystic, but that he was both
these things at the same time. In one way or another this seeming contrariety
was to remain with him throughout his life. There was always a part of him
that was the antisentimentalist, skeptic, "realist," and "scientist when I was
four years old." There was another part of him that was ever the mystic, the
poet, the rhapsodist, the seer of "wonderful vistas" who could be shamelessly
moved to tears by beauty, joy, and tragedy. The great risk that a man runs
when he is host to two such contrary tendencies of personality is that he will
embrace one tendency in the extreme and then set about to persecute all signs
of the other with the fervor of a reformed sinner. True, there was something
of the reformed sinner in Maslow's zealous undergraduate atheism, but,
taking his life on balance, it is fair to say that he avoided the pitfall remark-
ably well. His aim, especially in his mature years, was always to integrate the
two tendencies—or, as he might have said, to render them "synergic." Of
course, achievement and aim do not always coincide, and so it was on occasion with Maslow. This, however, serves only to remind us that a man's reach
often exceeds his grasp. Otherwise, as Browning put it, "What's a heaven
for?"

There is another point to be made as well. Before Maslow became a
psychologist—even before he had decided on psychology as a career—he was
already quite convinced that there are "wonderful possibilities and inscrutable depths in mankind." He was convinced, too, that a man could devote
himself to no higher task than that of "round[ing] out a larger, more wonderful conception of the greatness of the human species and the wonderful vistas
of progress just faintly glimpsed against the future." Thus the turning that
took place in his life in the late 1930s is best seen as a turning back to these
earlier, deeper, more abiding tendencies of mind. Of course, much had happened to him between the late 1920s and the late 1930s. Not only was he ten
years older and wiser, but also he had known the rigors and discipline of
graduate education and experimental science. Nonetheless, turn back he
surely did; and this time, as we have already indicated, he set out on the path
with a sense of mission and urgency.

So it was that Maslow's style thereafter was never that of the Talmudic commentator, the scrupulous citer of sources and drawer of fine distinctions. Neither was it the style of that romantic but wholly nonexistent "scientist" who never permits himself an opinion until "all the data are in" and who even then accepts the opinion only provisionally. His, for better or worse, was the style of a man who felt he had a great deal of truth to impart to the world and who, perceiving that life is short, could scarcely take time out for the conventional amenities. Whatever might have been Maslow's virtues and shortcomings, he was in any case a man of great passion and honesty. Perhaps at times his passion took the form of arrogance; perhaps, too, his honesty sometimes looked like naïveté. But throughout it all he was a man who took himself, his work, and the world around him with utter ingenuous seriousness. His early paper on Emerson was only the first of a great many instances in which he abhorred, or loved, or studied, or sought after something with all the vehemence that was in him.

2

Human Motivation

People are all decent underneath. All that is
necessary to prove this is to find out what the
motives are for their superficial behavior—
nasty, mean, or vicious though that behavior
may be. Once these motives are understood,
it is impossible to resent the behavior that
follows.—A. H. Maslow, Unpublished Note,
1938.

In the psychology of human motivation, the fundamental question
is simply this: Why do people behave as they do? For Maslow the question
led off in an especially difficult direction, for he began his inquiries by believing an especially difficult thing—namely, that "people are all decent underneath." Accordingly, the task before him was that of explaining why it is that
people often seem not to be decent at all.

The earliest record of Maslow's explicitly addressing himself to this
task is an unpublished note dated June 1938. He began with the passage that
we have already quoted and then continued:

Nasty behavior there is obviously. The only question is, why does such
behavior occur? Most people think vicious behavior comes from vicious
people. This is untrue. Others think that people are mean because they
themselves expect meanness from others. This is more true. Why is it that
people behave badly? Why are they cruel and bad? In a word, it is because
they are not liked. The insecurity cycle—from this flows everything. First of
all, suspicion and mistrust, loss of self-esteem with attempts to compensate.
If you don't like me, you may and probably will hurt me even more than you
have already merely by not liking me. If you hurt me, I'll hurt you first. The
person who behaves badly behaves so because of hurt, actual and expected,
and lashes out in self-defense, as a cornered animal might.

Here, then, was Maslow's first answer to the question: People are "nasty, mean, or vicious" not because they are wicked but because they are unloved, low in self-esteem, and insecure. And so it was that he could conclude as he began:

> The fact is that people are good, if only their fundamental wishes are satis-fied, their wishes for affection and security. Give people affection and secu-rity, and they will give affection and be secure in their feelings and behavior.

Maslow was confident of the conclusion, even though he recognized that it all sounded "positively mystic and sentimental." He also recognized the further question to which the conclusion led: "Does this mean," he asked with a certain wide-eyed wonderment, "that unselfishness is instinctive? Freud says the id is *completely* selfish. This I do not think. The tendency to affection is there as strongly as the hostile tendencies (except maybe in the neurotics Freud studied)."

There would seem to be two sources of Maslow's preoccupation at this time in his life with security and self-esteem. The first of these lay in the fact that he was himself no stranger to insecurity and low self-esteem; indeed, he had been intimately acquainted with both. As a child he had come to see himself as both unloved and unlovable, mainly because of what he thought to be his abyssmal ugliness. In his high school diaries he recorded, along with much "objective" self-recrimination, that his father had said aloud, half in earnest, at a family gathering, "Have you ever seen anyone uglier than Abe?" He also recorded during his first and only courtship how utterly amazed he was that his wife-to-be could even like, much less love, such an ugly and worthless person as himself. Even as he approached thirty, in the late 1930s, he sought partially to conceal his supposed ugliness by growing a moustache, which he kept ever after. Instances could be multiplied, but these will surely suffice to make the point.

The second source of Maslow's preoccupation with security and self-esteem may be found more near-at-hand in his then-current studies of dominance. As we have already mentioned, his studies of dominance in primates led, in the late 1930s, to research on dominance at the human level. In his earlier studies he had suggested that dominance behavior in primates is the result of a kind of "attitude of confidence" or "dominance-feeling." The connection between the two seemed fairly direct and uncomplicated, and so he found little need to distinguish carefully between them. In his later studies of human dominance, however, he found the distinction to be essential. His first published account along these lines appeared in 1937 (the year before the unpublished note with which we began) under the title "Dominance-Feeling, Behavior, and Status."[1] The main point he sought to make in this paper was

---

[1] A. H. Maslow, "Dominance-Feeling, Behavior, and Status," *Psychological Review,* 1937, **44**, 404–429.

that one must distinguish very carefully indeed at the human level between dominance-feeling and dominance behavior; for here it happens that one frequently encounters dominance behavior in the very *absence* of dominance-feeling. In these instances the dominance behavior is not so much "natural" dominance—in later years he would probably have called it healthy dominance or B-dominance—as it is a *compensation* for the lack of dominance-feeling.

Already in this paper of 1937 it is clear that what Maslow meant by the phrase "dominance-feeling" was a great deal broader than what would normally be suggested by the word "dominance." Its near synonyms included no fewer than the following: "(1) self-confidence, (2) self-esteem, (3) high self-respect and evaluation of self, (4) consciousness or feeling of 'superiority' in a very general sense, (5) forcefulness of personality, (6) strength of character, (7) a feeling of sureness with respect to other people, (8) a feeling of being able to handle other people, (9) a feeling of masterfulness and mastery, (10) a feeling that others do and ought to admire and respect one, (11) a feeling of general capability, (12) an absence of shyness, timidity, self-consciousness, or embarrassment, (13) a feeling of pride." Maslow recognized that "dominance" was perhaps not the best word to use, and he even suggested (in a footnote) that a better substitute might be "high ego-level." Still, he was inclined to retain "dominance" in order to make "the animal work continuous with work for children and adult human beings." By the next year he was beginning, at least in his unpublished notes, to write "security" and "self-esteem" in place of "dominance-feeling." In the early 1940s the change appeared in his published writings as well. Thus in 1940 he published a paper whose title contained the phrase "dominance-feeling" followed by the parenthesized explanation "self-esteem."[2] Two years later he was writing it the other way around: "self-esteem (dominance-feeling)."[3] Thereafter "dominance-feeling" dropped away entirely.

In any case, it is not difficult to imagine the course that Maslow's thoughts might have taken following his "Dominance-Feeling, Behavior, and Status" of 1937. Already he had noted that "compensatory dominance" is most readily distinguishable from "natural dominance" in those cases in which it is extreme or, as it were, *"over*-compensatory." For here the behavior is not so much dominant as domineering, "with antagonism to others, willfulness, impoliteness, selfishness, aggressiveness, tyrannizing, etc." It is a sham, a mere counterfeit, and it is apt to give the observer exactly this

impression of being strained and unnatural. It is more aggressive and louder than seems to be appropriate to the situation. It is in some cases even apt to be somewhat vulgar, and may sometimes also give the observer the impres-

[2] A. H. Maslow, "A Test for Dominance-Feeling (Self-Esteem) in College Women." *Journal of Social Psychology*, 1940, **12**, 255–270.
[3] A. H. Maslow, "Self-Esteem (Dominance-Feeling) and Sexuality in Women," *Journal of Social Psychology*, 1942, **16**, 259–294.

sion of expressing defiance or a chip-on-the-shoulder attitude, rather than calm assurance. . . . In other instances the compensatory behavior [may take] the form of apparent snobbishness with haughty, cold, aloof behavior.

From here it was surely not a long jump to the conclusion that everything that is "nasty, mean, or vicious" in human behavior is precisely this—an over-compensatory attempt to achieve security and self-esteem. Conversely, were it not for this crippling effect of insecurity and low self-esteem, there would be no wickedness in human behavior at all.

Toward the end of 1938 we find Maslow pursuing this line of thought once again, but this time with the aid of

my new notion of Fundamental or Natural Personality. . . . Proposition: That human beings are at birth and today deep down, secure and with good self-esteem, to be analogized with the Blackfoot Indian or the chimpanzee or the baby or the secure adult. And then societies *do* something to this Natural Personality, twist it, shape it, repress it.

He recounted that this conception of "natural personality" had only recently "fallen into structure" for him during a conversation with another young psychologist, Rod Menzies. He was describing to the latter his discovery that a certain woman, when hypnotized, exhibited a "dissociated" secondary personality. This woman's ordinary waking personality was characteristically low in self-esteem and security, whereas her secondary, trance personality was consistently higher in both. As he was describing the phenomenon, it suddenly came to him

that this was like stripping away a veneer to find out what really lay underneath. And lots of other hitherto-percolating thoughts came up to help and join in. My baby, whom I had observed with so much awe and wonder as a perfectly secure being; Wertheimer's remark that adults were deteriorated and spoiled children; that in primates we find these same patterns; that in my clinical work I have always found that *anyone,* however nasty and perverted and neurotic, was really sweet and loving and nice underneath, and that the only postulate I had to make in treating them was that they didn't get as much love as they wanted; that it was easier for me to make people more secure and higher in dominance [in clinical work] than to make secure ones insecure and high-dominance people into low-dominance people. And the conclusion followed . . . that there is more inertia in one direction than in the other, and therefore that one is more fundamental or natural than the other.[4]

Thus, once again, man is basically good; it is only life's pressures and frustrations that make him seem, all too often, otherwise. This view, of course, was not an altogether new one. It was akin, for example, to the view

[4]Unpublished note, December 1938.

of Pelagius, church father and heretic who denied the doctrine of original sin. It was akin also to the view propounded by the eighteenth-century Enlightenment. Indeed, in one form or another it had recurred throughout history. Nonetheless, it is fairly certain that Maslow had not encountered the view through any of these classical statements of it. He probably did soak up a certain amount of it from the popular socialism of the 1920s and 1930s, with which he flirted for a time; but for the most part he seems to have arrived at it quite independently (he certainly *thought* he had arrived at it independently). This historical isolation was perhaps a weakness, but it was also a great strength. For in believing himself to be the first ever to have thought of it, he was able to embark on the task wholeheartedly, his vision unclouded by earlier attempts, successes, and failures. And so he was able to write, with his characteristic mixture of innocence and audacity:

> Generally, the picture I have now is *such* a vague one, but with such intimations of immortality, with such great flashes of hope playing around it, that I have the feeling we're on the edge of a great human revolution . . . like the Copernican or the Darwinian ones. But there are so many things to consider, and they are so unformed, and it is so difficult to fit them into a structure. Well, we'll try.[5]

In seeking to fit all these thoughts "into a structure," one thing must have seemed clear to Maslow from the very beginning—namely, that his view was sharply at variance with the mainstream of psychological opinion. For not only was it apt to seem "positively mystic and sentimental," but its basic tenet simply flew in the face of many assumptions that the psychology of the time held to be all but self-evident. We shall have no difficulty recognizing those assumptions, for the psychological mainstream has changed little from that time to this. If, in the late 1930s, one had set about to find a view of human nature that had a kind of official status within American psychology, he would have found two powerful contenders for the role. The first was behaviorism, especially of the sort then being worked out by Clark Hull and his associates; the second was that relatively new import from abroad, psychoanalysis. These two "isms" had their differences, to be sure, but they also had their points of agreement. And not the least of these would have been their resounding denials—each in its own way—of the assertion that "people are all decent underneath."

Of the two views, it is the psychoanalytic that would have denied Maslow's assertion the more strongly (even though this was the "ism" from which he felt he had learned the most). For at the very heart of the psychoanalytic doctrine lay the assumption that people are not the least bit "decent underneath." Quite the contrary, what people are underneath is a

---

[5]Unpublished note, December 1938.

kind of seething, mindless chaos of selfish, erotic, and destructive impulses. Fortunately, these impulses are fairly successfully controlled by internal inhibitions and societal restraints; otherwise, human behavior would be a good deal more "nasty, mean, or vicious" than it already is.

The behavioristic doctrine would have been milder in its rejection of the assertion, but no less resolute. It would have run somewhat as follows: Although it cannot be said that man is basically wicked, neither can it be said that he is basically good. The best we can say is that he is neither one nor the other, but neutral. All of man's behavior is learned, and that learning takes place in every instance as a result of "reinforcement." If a man receives reinforcement for doing what we call "good," then "good" is what he will do. The same is true for what we call "evil": if he receives reinforcement for doing it, he will learn it; and if he learns it, he will do it. But in neither case can we speak of a "natural personality" that is either inherently good or inherently evil. (Actually, by the end of the 1930s several of the chief proponents of the behavioristic doctrine *were* inclining a bit toward the psychoanalytic view of inherent evil. We speak here of the behavioristic "frustration-aggression hypothesis," which held that frustration necessarily results in aggression, either directly expressed against the perceived frustrating agent or else displaced or sublimated.)[6]

Both of these mainstream psychological doctrines of human nature rested on a theory of motivation. Freud's psychoanalytic view held that all human motives could be listed under one or the other of two headings: they belong either to the self-preservative instincts (the "ego instincts") or to the erotic instincts. Freud of course recognized that many ostensible human motives do not seem to belong to either of these categories; but this, he considered, is simply because we do not look deep enough. There are certain of these instinctive impulses—namely, the erotic—that cannot be satisfied directly and openly except at the risk of punishment and pain. Thus, if they are to be satisfied at all, as they must, they must be acted on secretly and indirectly. The result is that every effort is made to conceal their true identity, their true source and aim, from both the person himself and those who might be observing him. Small wonder, then, that people sometimes give the appearance of being "decent," for such is precisely the function of almost all those processes that Freud spoke of as "mechanisms of defense." Their task is that of making the worse cause seem the better cause and thus of giving vice the appearance of virtue. But we must remember that it is an appearance and nothing more. If we look sufficiently beneath the surface, through the lens of psychoanalysis, we shall see soon enough that all human behavior results from instinctual impulses that are either erotic or self-preservative. (In a later revision of his views, Freud considered that the self-preservative instincts

[6]J. Dollard, L. W. Doob, N. E. Miller, O. H. Mowrer, and R. R. Sears, *Frustration and Aggression* (New Haven, Conn.: Yale University Press, 1939).

were but special cases of the erotic instincts; at the same time, he enlarged his scheme of motivation with the addition of a new category of instinct, the so-called death instinct.)

Freud's argument, in other words, was that we must carefully distinguish those few human motives that are deep and real—the self-preservative, the erotic, and later the destructive—from all those others that are only superficial and apparent. He also held that the superficial motives are in some sense *derivative* of the deeper ones. The behavioristic theory argued for a similar distinction: In any animal species there are certain "drives" that may be spoken of as *primary*, inasmuch as they are inborn and abiding. Their common characteristic is that they all depend on innate physiological need. Thus, in the human species, the primary drives would include hunger, thirst, sex, the need for oxygen, and the like—all those drives that a wag once described as "gut drives." Then there is another class of drives. These are all acquired through learning and are thus best spoken of as *secondary*. Take, for example, the often encountered human drive to accumulate money. This is clearly an acquired drive, and it is acquired only insofar as it is instrumental to the satisfaction of a primary drive such as hunger. The same would hold true for all other nonprimary drives—for love, status, success, or whatever. They are all derivative of the gut drives. If there is an intrinsic human nature, then, its fundamental goals are simply these: to fill the belly, to slake thirst, to find a suitable sexual object in time of need, and so on—in short, to survive and propagate in good Darwinian fashion. All else, be it good or evil, is *extrinsic*, a mere accretion.

Our allusion to "good Darwinian fashion" is no accident, for, if there was anything sacred to psychology during the period between, say, 1890 and 1940, it was Darwinian and neo-Darwinian evolutionary theory. Both of the mainstream psychological doctrines that we have mentioned were laced with assumptions that were Darwinian through and through. And chief among these was the assumption concerning motivation that we have just encountered: that the innate, intrinsic motivational constitution of a species can consist only of drives that conduce either to the survival of the individual or to the propagation of the species—in short, self-preservation and sex. Once this assumption is accepted, it is clear that any assertion about the basic goodness of human nature, intrinsic human decency, and the like must be summarily rejected. Conversely, in order to accept such an assertion, one would have to reject, or at least modify, the underlying Darwinian assumption. Maslow probably did not conceive of the task in just this way, but that is what it amounted to all the same.

The task was both begun and completed in two papers that Maslow published in 1943. In the first of these, "A Preface to Motivation Theory,"[7] he appeared for the most part to be groping. He obviously thought that

[7]A. H. Maslow, "A Preface to Motivation Theory." *Psychosomatic Medicine,* 1943, **5,** 85–92.

something was fundamentally wrong with the psychology of motivation, but he seemed to have no clear view of what might be done, overall, to set things aright. The result was a rather unsystematic collection of criticisms and recommendations, each individually sound and well drawn, but as a whole no greater than the sum of its parts. It was apparently only after he had written this first paper that he saw how one of its recommendations could be used not just to refurbish the psychology of motivation but to renovate it from bottom to top. This recommendation had appeared rather inconspicuously in the paper under the heading "Relationships of Motivations." It had a kind of common-sense obviousness about it that made it even more inconspicuous. "Man is a wanting animal," he wrote,

> and rarely reaches a state of complete satisfaction except for a short time. As one desire is satisfied, another pops up to take its place. When this is satisfied, still another comes into the foreground, etc. It is characteristic of the human being that he is practically always desiring something.

But it is important to note that these desires do not succeed one another willy-nilly. On the contrary, there is a readily discernible sense and order to their succession. Why is it then, that the later desires do not appear until the earlier ones have been satisfied? It is simply that the earlier motives are more basic, more fundamental, or, as Maslow put it, "prepotent." For clearly

> we should never have the desire to compose music or create mathematical systems, or to adorn our homes, or to be well dressed if our stomachs were empty most of the time, or if we were continually dying of thirst, or if we were continually threatened by an always impending catastrophe, or if everyone hated us.[8]

Here we have an example of one of Maslow's greatest virtues as a psychologist—namely, his ability to wrest something of psychological value from a commonplace. Certainly there was nothing novel about the observation that one almost never runs short of desires—nor in the observation that the mind does not fly to higher things on an empty stomach. But there was something very novel indeed in what Maslow saw as the theoretical implication of these two commonplaces. In the earlier paper, "A Preface to Motivation Theory," he carried it only part way: his only conclusion was that needs, drives, motives, desires, or what have you "seem to arrange themselves in some sort of hierarchy of prepotency." In his slightly later "Theory of Human Motivation,"[9] however, the implication appeared full-blown. He began the

[8]A. H. Maslow, *Motivation and Personality* (New York: Harper & Brothers, 1954), p. 69.
[9]A. H. Maslow, "A Theory of Human Motivation." *Psychological Review,* 1943, **50,** 370–396.

paper on what must have seemed an entirely orthodox note; that is, he affirmed at the outset that any theory of motivation must surely begin with the physiological needs—the gut drives—survival and sex. But to a discerning reader it would have become clear fairly soon that, when Maslow spoke of the physiological needs as being "the starting point of motivation theory," what he had in mind was something quite different from the conventional understanding of the matter. In both the psychoanalytic and the behavioristic theories, Maslow's admission that "these physiological needs are [undoubtedly] the most prepotent of all" could have meant only one thing—namely, that all other motives are in some fashion *derived* from the physiological needs. Maslow, quite to the contrary, was suggesting that these other motives —some of them at least—are not derived from the physiological needs at all; rather, they are innate, built-in, biologically given, and the role of the physiological needs is nothing other than to *inhibit* their expression. This, then, is the full meaning of Maslow's phrase "hierarchy of prepotency":

> It is quite true that man lives by bread alone—when there is no bread. But what happens to man's desires when there *is* plenty of bread and when his belly is chronically filled? *At once other (and higher) needs emerge,* and these, rather than physiological hungers, dominate the organism. And when these in turn are satisfied, again new (and still higher) needs emerge, and so on.[10]

If the physiological needs are the most prepotent of motives, what then are the next most prepotent? Putting it another way, once the physiological needs have been fairly well satisfied, as they normally are in our society, what then are the next motives to emerge? This next most prepotent class of motives includes what Maslow spoke of as the "safety needs," of which

> all that has been said of the physiological needs is equally true, although in less degree. . . . The organism may equally well be wholly dominated by them. They may serve as the almost exclusive organizers of behavior, recruiting all the capacities of the organism in their service, and we may then fairly describe the whole organism as a safety-seeking mechanism.[11]

Maslow went on to observe, however, that "the healthy, normal, fortunate adult in our culture is largely satisfied in his safety needs" and, thus, that "if we wish to see these needs directly and clearly, we must turn to neurotic or near-neurotic individuals, and to the economic and social underdogs. It is true, of course, that we find normal expressions of the safety needs in such

[10] *Motivation and Personality,* p. 83. In later years Maslow spoke of these "new (and still higher) needs" under the heading of "meta-motivation." It is also what he had in mind when he spoke of "grumbles," "grumble theory," and "meta-grumbles." His notion throughout was that, as lower needs, discontents, or "grumbles" are put to rest, they will inevitably be supplanted by higher ones.

[11] *Motivation and Personality,* p. 376.

phenomena as the common preference for a job with tenure and protection, the desires for a savings account, and for insurance of various kinds." We also find them in "the very common preference for familiar rather than unfamiliar things," in "the tendency to have some religion or world philosophy that organizes the universe and the men in it into some sort of satisfactorily coherent, meaningful whole," and even in "science and philosophy in general." For the most part, though, "the need for safety is seen as an active and dominant mobilizer of the [person's] resources only in emergencies, e.g., war, disease, natural catastrophes, crime waves, societal disorganization, neurosis, brain injury, chronically bad situations."[12]

Once the safety needs have been fairly well satisfied, there emerge yet other needs, the needs for "belongingness and love," and the whole cycle will then

> repeat itself with this new center. Now the person will feel keenly, as never before, the absence of friends, or a sweetheart, or a wife, or children. He will hunger for affectionate relations with people in general, namely, for a place in his group, and he will strive with great intensity to achieve this goal. He will want to attain such a place more than anything else in the world and may even forget that once, when he was hungry, he sneered at love as unreal or unnecessary or unimportant.[13]

These needs for belongingness and love are of course less prepotent than either the physiological needs or the safety needs, but they are "basic needs" nonetheless. That is, they are inherent in the biological constitution of the species, and they will inevitably rise to the motivational surface once all other more prepotent needs have been fairly well satisfied. There is, however, one important respect in which the needs for belongingness and love differ quite sharply from the other two classes of needs that we have spoken of. As we have noted, the physiological needs and the safety needs are normally fairly well satisfied in our culture; the belongingness and love needs, on the other hand, are not. This is so because "love and affection, as well as their possible expressions in sexuality, are generally looked upon with ambivalence and are customarily hedged about with many restrictions and inhibitions." Thus it is that "in our society the thwarting of these needs is the most commonly found core in cases of maladjustment and more severe psychopathology."[14]

Insofar as the belongingness and love needs *are* satisfied, however, there will emerge still another class of basic needs, the "esteem needs." These consist in the

> need or desire for a stable, firmly based, usually high evaluation of [oneself] . . . and may therefore be classified into two subsidiary sets. . . . First [there

---

[12] *Motivation and Personality*, pp. 87–88.
[13] *Motivation and Personality*, p. 89.
[14] *Motivation and Personality*, pp. 89–90.

is] the desire for strength, for achievement, for adequacy, for mastery and competence, for confidence in the face of the world, and for independence and freedom. Second, we have what we may call the desire for reputation or prestige . . ., status, dominance, recognition, attention, importance, or appreciation.[15]

Like the belongingness and love needs, the esteem needs are less commonly satisfied in our society than are either of the two more prepotent classes of needs.

Up to this point the orthodox psychoanalyst or behaviorist of the day might have found much to disagree with in Maslow's "Theory of Human Motivation," but he would not have found it altogether repugnant. On the subject of the physiological needs, for example, there would have been almost complete accord in all camps: that the physiological needs are "basic" is simply indisputable. Of course, on the subject of "safety," "love and belongingness," and "esteem," there would have been less accord, for, although both orthodoxies admitted the existence of such needs, they naturally saw them as being derived rather than basic (except insofar as "love" included "sex"). All the same, they would probably have maintained a sporting tolerance for Maslow's attempt, for it was after all a rather clever one. To wit, one of the principal reasons why psychological theorists had been unwilling to regard nonphysiological needs as basic is that the nonphysiological needs are not nearly so widely characteristic of the species as are the physiological. Thus, we may say that hunger is a basic need because almost any person deprived of food long enough will seek it. The same can be said to a lesser degree of safety, but of belongingness-love and esteem it can scarcely be said at all. Many indeed are the persons—if not in our own culture then in others —for whom love and esteem are negligible considerations at most. Maslow, on the other hand, was arguing that these needs are less often found in the species not because they are less basic, but rather because they are less prepotent. In effect, he was arguing that, in a world where all physiological and safety needs were fully satisfied, the need for belongingness and love would be as widely characteristic of the species as hunger is in this world. It is somewhat analogous to the relationship between, say, the need for oxygen and the need for food. Both are physiological needs and undeniably basic, but it is the need for oxygen that is the more prepotent. Thus, if an extremely hungry man is suddenly deprived of oxygen, his hunger motive will vanish —as though it had never existed—until such time as the need for oxygen has been satisfied. And this, Maslow argued, is precisely what happens in the case of belongingness-love and esteem: they are basic needs to be sure, but they become manifest only insofar as other, more prepotent, needs are satisfied. Of course, the orthodox psychoanalysts and behaviorists might not have

[15] *Motivation and Personality*, p. 90.

found the argument convincing, but the better among them could scarcely refuse to respect its virtuosity.

Beyond this point, however, Maslow embarked on a course that the two great orthodoxies of the day must sooner or later have found very questionable indeed, for, if the theory did not already seem "positively mystic and sentimental," it was bound to seem so now. We refer, of course, to the hypothesis of "self-actualization" and to all the many pathways down which it eventually led. In the next chapter we shall try to retrace the steps by which Maslow arrived at this notion, and later still we shall consider what he thought to be some of its more important involvements and implications. For the moment, though, let us simply see what role he assigned to it in his 1943 "Theory of Human Motivation." Even after all other more prepotent needs (physiological, safety, belongingness-love, esteem) have been satisfied, he wrote,

> we may still often (if not always) expect that a new discontent and restlessness will develop, unless the individual is doing what he is fitted for. A musician must make music, an artist must paint, a poet must write, if he is to be ultimately at peace with himself. What a man *can* be, he *must* be. This need we may call self-actualization. ... It refers to man's desire for self-fulfillment, namely, to the tendency for him to become actualized in what he is potentially. This tendency might be phrased as the desire to become more and more what one is, to become everything that one is capable of becoming.[16]

The extent to which Maslow would be preoccupied with this notion in later years was hardly hinted at by the very few words he used to describe it in 1943. As we shall see later, the reason he did not say more about it at this time is simply that he had nothing more to say. It was not until 1945, two years after his first published mention of self-actualization, that he set about systematically to explore the idea and (if you will) the phenomenon.

Let us now back up a bit and see what we have. In his private ruminations of 1938, Maslow had written: "The fact is that people are good, if only their fundamental wishes are satisfied"—their wishes for security, love, and esteem. Now he was writing, in effect: "The fact is that people are self-actualizing, if only their basic needs are satisfied"—their needs for safety, love, and esteem, not to mention the most basic of all, their physiological needs. Earlier he had written: "People are all decent underneath"; they at times seem otherwise only because they are *lacking* in security, love, and self-esteem. Now he was writing, in effect: "People are all self-actualizing underneath"; they at times seem otherwise only because their more prepotent needs (safety, love, esteem) have *not* been adequately satisfied. We need

---

[16]*Motivation and Personality*, pp. 91–92.

hardly go on to show that Maslow's "good underneath" of 1938 was the direct ancestor of his "self-actualization" of 1943. As we shall see in the next chapter, he was himself accustomed to using the phrases "self-actualization" and "good human being" fairly interchangeably in the early and middle 1940s.

Of course, this "people are all decent underneath" implication was not drawn out in just these terms in his motivation paper of 1943 (it was written, after all, for the *Psychological Review*), but it was at least hinted at. At the very end of the paper, Maslow put forward

> the bold postulation that a man who is thwarted in any of his basic needs may fairly be envisaged simply as a sick man. This is a fair parallel to our designation as "sick" of the man who lacks vitamins or minerals. Who is to say that a lack of love is less important than a lack of vitamins? Since we know the pathogenic effects of love starvation, who is to say that we are invoking value-questions in an unscientific or illegitimate way, any more than the physician does who diagnoses and treats pellagra or scurvy? If I were permitted this usage, I should then say simply that a healthy man is primarily motivated by his needs to develop and actualize his fullest poten-tialities and capacities. If a man has any other basic needs in any active, chronic sense, then he is simply an unhealthy man. He is as surely sick as if he had suddenly developed a strong salt hunger or calcium hunger.[17]

Thus, to be healthy is to be good and self-actualizing, and if one falls short of being good and self-actualizing, he does so only because he is sick. This, of course, is not to say that people are all good and self-actualizing; it is only to say that they are all good and self-actualizing *underneath.* If only their basic needs are adequately fulfilled, they would be good and self-actualizing on the surface as well.

Ever since Darwin's *Origin of Species* of 1859, it had been easy to see how a provident (if mindless) nature had contrived to ensure that the physio-logical needs of a species—hunger, thirst, sex, and the like—would be basic, innate, built-in, biologically given. For it is precisely these needs that conduce to the survival of the individual and the propagation of the species. A respect-able Darwinian case could also be made for what Maslow called the "safety needs," for it is not difficult to see that these, too, would have biological survival value and thus be "naturally selected" in the evolution of the species. When we come to "belongingness and love," the matter becomes more diffi-cult, though still not impossible. That is, even here one could argue that the social behavior to which such a class of needs might lead would have biologi-cal survival value and thus be retained through natural selection as an innate disposition of the species. With "esteem," however, the evolutionary ob-struction becomes all but insurmountable. There is simply no neat, uncon-

[17]"Theory of Human Motivation," pp. 393–394.

voluted way of arguing that an innate need for esteem would have biological survival value—at least not in the conventional Darwinian or neo-Darwinian sense of the term. And it surely goes without saying that the case for "self-actualization" would be more difficult still. Maslow, for better or worse, was unperturbed by these considerations. His attitude throughout seems to have been this: if the facts as I see them do not comport with established theory, then so much the worse for established theory. It was the attitude that he seemed to express in the concluding paragraph of his "Theory of Human Motivation," where he forewarned the reader: "If this statement [about health and self-actualization] seems unusual or paradoxical ... be assured that this is only one among many such paradoxes that will appear as we revise our ways of looking at man's deeper motivations."[18] The reader of 1943, steeped as he was in the views of behaviorism on the one hand and psychoanalysis on the other, could hardly have guessed just *how* unusual or paradoxical!

[18]"Theory of Human Motivation," p. 395.

3

Self-Actualization

Ich lehre euch den Übermenschen. Der Mensch ist etwas, das überwunden werden soll. Was habt ihr getan, ihn zu überwinden?—Friedrich Nietzsche, *Also Sprach Zarathustra,* 1883.

("I teach you the Overman. Ordinary man is something to be surpassed. What have *you* done to surpass him?")

According to Maslow, his concept of self-actualization[1] arose from "the effort of a young intellectual to try to understand [two persons] whom he loved, adored, and admired and who were very, very wonderful people." These two persons were Ruth Benedict and Max Wertheimer, both of whom he had come to know in New York City in the late 1930s. He went on to relate that he kept notes on Benedict and Wertheimer and that, in the middle of his note keeping, the concept of self-actualization suddenly came to him as in a flash:

> I realized in one wonderful moment that their two patterns could be generalized. I was talking about a kind of person, not about two noncomparable individuals. There was wonderful excitement in this. I tried to see whether this pattern could be found elsewhere, and I did find it elsewhere, in one person after another.[2]

This account of the origins of the self-actualization concept is certainly true as far as it goes, but it is not the whole story. For one thing, it fails

[1]Maslow got the term "self-actualization" from Kurt Goldstein, who had used it in quite a different sense. Goldstein was never entirely pleased with the use to which Maslow put the term.

[2]A. H. Maslow, *The Farther Reaches of Human Nature* (New York: Viking Press, 1971), pp. 41–42.

to mention how very thoroughly the stage was already set for the events described. As we have just seen, Maslow had long been convinced that human nature holds "wonderful possibilities and inscrutable depths" and that it is basically good. Perhaps Benedict and Wertheimer were the first to appear to him as living confirmations of these beliefs; perhaps in them, too, he found the first hope of giving his beliefs an empirical leg to stand on. All the same, the beliefs were there long before Maslow ever met Benedict or Wertheimer, and his attempt to understand these "very, very wonderful people" did not arise in a vacuum. Neither did his one wonderful moment of realization.

Another omission has to do with what came afterward. Maslow's account leaves us with the impression that the self-actualization concept came upon him full-born, in a single blinding moment of illumination. Doubtless it did come in such a moment, but it did not come full-born. Rather, it developed gradually over the period of about a decade. We would not dwell further on the matter except that this inaccurate impression was abetted on at least one other occasion. Thus, Maslow's study of Benedict and Wertheimer dated from the early 1940s—certainly from before 1943, when his first published mention of self-actualization appeared in "Theory of Human Motivation." His initial paper on self-actualization ("Self-Actualization: A Study of Psychological Health")[3] appeared in 1950; then, four years later, when he republished the paper in his book *Motivation and Personality,* he declared that he had actually written it "about 1943" but had held it back for seven years while he "summoned up enough courage to print it."[4] The statement comports nicely with the impression mentioned above, but it is difficult to reconcile with the surviving records. It is probably to be credited to the poor memory for detail from which Maslow felt he suffered throughout his life. At any rate, the earliest pertinent record happens to date from just that year, 1943, and it suggests that the characteristics of the self-actualizing person as Maslow then saw them were a far cry indeed from the ones he portrayed in his paper of 1950. They were, in fact, rather bland by comparison: ". . . peace, contentment, calmness, the full utilization of capacities, full creativity and the like . . . [and] success of interpersonal relationships."[5] Certainly his thoughts on self-actualization at that time were leading in the direction of his 1950 paper, but it is hard to believe that the paper had yet been written or even that it was anywhere near being written. The earliest record we have of Maslow's drafting a paper on self-actualization dates from

[3] A. H. Maslow, "Self-Actualization: A Study of Psychological Health." In *Personality Symposia* (New York: Grune & Stratton, 1950), pp. 11–34.
[4] A. H. Maslow, *Motivation and Personality* (New York: Harper & Brothers, 1954), p. xiii.
[5] Unpublished description of a course in the psychology of personality that Maslow was then teaching at Brooklyn College.

1946, and even as late as 1949 he recorded that he was still "writing up self-actualization stuff for publication."[6] All in all, the surviving records indicate that the vision of self-actualization presented in the paper of 1950 was still aborning as late as 1947, and perhaps even as late as 1949, Maslow's later recollection of the events notwithstanding.

The "Good Human Being" Notebook

But if Maslow's poor memory was at times a curse for him, it was also a blessing for us, for its result was that he usually kept very thorough notes and records. The records of his pre-1950 work on self-actualization are not so complete as we might wish, but they are sufficient to allow us to reconstruct at least the major outlines of the work. We shall be relying chiefly on a notebook that Maslow began keeping in 1945 as a record of what he called his "GHB" (Good Human Being) research. He kept the notebook off and on between 1945 and 1949, and it is without question the fullest record of his early research and reflection on self-actualization that survives. It is presented almost in its entirety in the Appendix.

Maslow began his GHB notebook because he had reached a decision. Heretofore his work on self-actualization had been directed almost entirely toward "studying self-actualized adults over fifty or sixty and then getting a list of their common characteristics."[7] It had been a rather informal study, to say the least. As he noted in his 1950 paper, it consisted

> not so much in the usual gathering of specific and discrete facts as in the slow development of a global or holistic impression of the sort that we form of our friends and acquaintances. It was rarely possible to set up a situation, to ask pointed questions, or to do any testing with my older subjects. . . . Contacts were fortuitous and of the ordinary social sort. Friends and relatives were questioned where this was possible.[8]

Maslow's decision, as he began his GHB notebook, was to supplement what he had done so far with something that more closely resembled conventional psychological research. Thus, he began his first entry, "after fussing along for some years I have decided to dig into GHB research and do it more formally and rigidly."

His plan was to study college students—not so much because he expected to find a high incidence of self-actualization among them, but simply because they were available and because he hoped that, in such a large

---

[6]GHB Notebook, April 1946, April 1949.
[7]All quotations in this section are from the GHB Notebook unless otherwise indicated.
[8]*Motivation and Personality,* p. 202.

sample of students as Brooklyn College afforded, he might find a few who at least approximated his criteria for self-actualization. "The layout," as he described it, was "to collect students who look like potential GHB and then go through several sieving processes, keeping records all the way." These sieving processes amounted to the following: first, he would "pick them out just by looking at them in class"; next, he would "look up their security scores"[9]; then he would "interview them for about an hour and ask them to write me a memorandum of the interview to the best of their memory for my records"; finally, he would administer the Rorschach test to them.

Maslow had apparently already selected and tested a few subjects by the time he made this first entry in the notebook, for he was even then aware that there were "lots of problems." One of these was that practically all the subjects whom he had so far selected gave poor results on the Rorschach test. He was understandably puzzled that subjects whom he regarded as potentially self-actualizing should perform poorly on a test designed to diagnose psychopathology. He lamented that he had been unable "to get any satisfaction on this from the experts" and went on to question "what's a good Rorschach [test result] anyway?" (His later conclusion on the matter was that the Rorschach test is "far more useful in revealing concealed psychopathology than in selecting healthy people."[10])

Another problem was that the subjects whom he had selected as potential self-actualizers often had low security scores, whereas those whom he had definitely rejected often had high ones. This too was puzzling, for he was convinced that security and self-esteem went arm-in-arm with self-actualization. In the next notebook entry he recorded what seemed to him the likely explanation: "I get the impression that the security test taps only superficial consciousness, which is sometimes contradicted by deeper, more unconscious security feelings."

Finally, Maslow was aware of a possible bias in his selections: "How come I pick so many more girls than boys," he asked himself, "and how come they're all very pretty?" More generally, he recognized that in research of this sort "the picker's values will certainly get in the way"—no matter who is doing the picking.

There are some who, confronted with these and other problems that attended the research, would have abandoned hope before they began. Maslow, however, was characteristically undaunted: "I try to be as conscious as possible of insurmountable difficulties," he wrote in the first entry of the notebook, "and then I go ahead anyway."

At least, he was undaunted at the beginning. In his 1950 paper on self-actualization Maslow alluded only very briefly to his research with col-

---

[9]A. H. Maslow, "A Test for Dominance-Feeling (Self-Esteem) in College Women," *Journal of Social Psychology*, 1940, **12**, 255–270.
[10]*Motivation and Personality*, p. 200.

lege students. He noted that its aim was "to choose the healthiest 1 percent of the college population," that it was "pursued over a two-year period as time permitted," and that it "had to be interrupted before completion." What he did not note is that the research amounted to a long and almost unbroken series of disappointments. Time and again in his notebook he made statements such as "——looks like a good GHB prospect," only to follow them days or weeks or months later with a retraction such as "——is definitely not GHB—smug, obnoxious, lazy, unambitious." The disappointment was compounded by the fact that his subjects' security scores and Rorschach performances—these being the two independent, objective measures on which he had pinned his research hopes—continued in their failure to produce usable data. Thus, even as early as November 1945 (he had begun the notebook in May), we find him confiding that "as the work goes on, my objectives shrink more and more."

Still he pressed on with it for two years and more. In December 1945 he made an entry in the notebook that seems to explain a great deal about what sustained him in the research even in the face of such repeated disappointment. He began by reporting a conversation he had recently had on the concept of original sin and then went on to consider what kind of a case might be made for the contrary concept of "original goodness." The greatest difficulty, he observed, is that we simply cannot find the answer to the question in "ordinary mankind." If we study only the ordinary person, we shall no more be able to prove original goodness than original sin. But what would happen, he went on to ask, if we began by studying "extraordinary people" (which he of course had already begun doing)?

> Certainly a visitor from Mars descending upon a colony of birth-injured cripples, dwarfs, hunchbacks, etc., could not deduce what they *should* have been. But then let us study not cripples, but the closest approach we can get to whole, healthy men. In them we find qualitative differences, a different system of motivation, emotion, value, thinking, and perceiving.

Indeed, Maslow went on to say, there is a certain sense in which these extraordinary, whole, healthy men are the *only* genuine representatives of mankind. All the others are but feeble, degenerate simulacra; they are but "sick, twisted cripples."

This was one of the very few occasions when Maslow spoke of "ordinary mankind" with something approaching contempt. In the next entry in the notebook he softened his opinion considerably. "The notion I am working toward," he wrote, "is of some ideal of human nature, closely approximated in reality by a few 'self-actualized' people." It is quite true that everyone else is sick and crippled "in greater or lesser degree," he continued, "but these degrees are much less important than we have thought." Indeed, the only real difference would seem to be that, whereas all persons at birth have the potential for self-actualization, "most all of them get it knocked out" before they have had the chance to develop it. The self-actualizing person, therefore, is not so much an ordinary man "with something added" as he is an ordinary man "with nothing taken away." The self-actualizing person is a full human being; the ordinary man is the same human being with "dampened and inhibited powers and capacities." The self-actualized person is, in short, "synonymous with human nature in general."

Thus, as Maslow saw it, to know self-actualization is to know human nature as it truly is and to know that it is basically good. Of course, Maslow had long been convinced that human nature is basically good, but now, with his GHB research, he had set out to prove it—that is, to provide it with empirical support. It was too high a purpose to abandon merely because of a few "insurmountable difficulties."

As we have said, however, hope and tenacity alone were not enough. What were needed were usable data, and these were not forthcoming. Thus, although the research was "of course very instructive at the clinical level," nothing ever really came of it. (In the 1950 paper Maslow wrote: "I had to conclude that self-actualization of the sort I had found in my older subjects was not possible in our society for young, developing people.") The result was that the GHB notebook, which began as a place for recording formal research work, was increasingly given over to continuing Maslow's earlier task of developing "a global or holistic impression."

Up to this point—toward the middle of 1945, let us say—Maslow's vision of self-actualization seems to have remained fairly unaltered from what it had been in 1943. It was then, we may recall, that he described the chief characteristics of the self-actualizing person as "peace, contentment, calmness, the full utilization of capacities, full creativity . . . [and] success of interpersonal relationships." By 1945 he had added good adjustment and absence of psychopathology to his "list of common characteristics," but otherwise there was nothing to suggest that his vision had changed in any fundamental way. The first indication of a change came about four months after Maslow had begun his GHB notebook. It had to do with what he spoke of in his 1950 paper as the self-actualizing person's "need for privacy." He had already noticed that the adult subjects whom he had studied were not eager to bare their souls to him, but it was only after working with his students that he definitely decided on this as a general characteristic of the self-actualizing person. "It finally becomes unmistakably clear," he wrote,

> that my subjects won't cooperate as they have in other studies. I learned long ago that the older GHBs had an awfully strong sense of privacy, as Ruth Benedict tried to explain to me long ago. She as a matter of fact spoke more freely than any of them about personal things. There was no difficulty about impersonal things, and they would go on at length about their ideas or theories . . . [But] they all seemed uneasy when I told them what I thought

of them and what I wanted of them. Now, to a lesser extent, I find the same with my college students, though probably for different reasons. They just seem bored or evasive or merely polite. I think all the talk and probing just bores them. It's a chore. If I get them in a corner, they'll kick through. They won't protest against it or refuse it; they just don't show up or come late or postpone. . . . It's gotten so that I think of all this as a GHB characteristic and suspect anyone who cooperates eagerly.

The explanation that Maslow offered for this need for privacy ran somewhat as follows: The self-actualizing person has nothing to gain by baring his soul —that is, he has no neurotic needs that would be satisfied by disclosing private matters. Accordingly, insofar as the self-actualizing person cooperates at all in responding to interviews and questionnaires, "it's pure and simple doing me a favor with little or no return." The same explanation appeared in the 1950 paper, though in less homely language.

The next addition to the list was perhaps also the most important, for it developed into what Maslow included in the 1950 paper as the very first characteristic of the self-actualizing person. It appeared for the first and only time in the notebook in a surprisingly brief entry of December 1945. "I have been thinking for some time," Maslow recorded,

> that an especially important characteristic of my GHBs is their ability to see reality more clearly. This showed itself in my security studies, especially among the Blackfoot Indians. It showed itself most—or at least first—in the ability to judge character. They could spot a phony a mile away.

This, of course, is what Maslow spoke of in the 1950 paper under the heading "more efficient perception of reality and more comfortable relations with it." There is no other surviving record of his pre-1950 thoughts on this important characteristic, so we shall not meet with it again until we consider how it was presented in the published paper. As with the preceding characteristic, we shall find that this one underwent considerable development between 1945 and 1950.

There were only two further characteristics of the self-actualizing person that appeared in the GHB notebook. The first came early in 1946 and was mentioned only very briefly. Maslow remarked, rather in passing, that he would "have to start writing eventually about the relation of these [self-actualizing] people to 'mystic experiences.' Any naturalistic definition of a mystic would be close to a definition of the self-actualized person. Also, the fact is that these people (or most of them) have many so-called mystic experiences only never call them that." The context of the remark does not indicate what might have precipitated it. Also, it is not clear whether Maslow was speaking of his older subjects, his college students, his "public and historical figures," or, indeed, all of them. In any case, let us recall that Maslow himself was certainly no stranger to the "mystic experience." In his

1950 paper he wrote that "because this experience is a natural experience, well within the jurisdiction of science, it is probably better to use Freud's term ... oceanic feeling." A few years later he coined an even more "naturalistic" name for it: "peak-experience."

The final characteristic appeared toward the middle of 1947. Maslow had at that time been reading a number of biographies in the hope of finding among them some instances of self-actualization. On the basis of those several cases that he thought he had found, he concluded that

> one characteristic to make much of is lack of cant. Also sense of humor, lack of fanaticism, tolerance of others, or whatever it is [whose absence] makes John Brown, Garrison, et al., so distasteful—or Daniel DeLeon, a typical fanatic who values dogma and theory more than men, the kind of man who can start crusades, inquisitions, purges, terrors.

It was perhaps this realization that spawned the paper he published in the following year under the title "Cognition of the Particular and the Generic."[11] In any event, the interpretation that he offered at this point in the notebook certainly foreshadowed the theme of the cognition paper. It was also clearly recognizable as an ancestor of some of the materials that appeared in the 1950 self-actualization paper. He began by reflecting on the fact that all of the communists of his acquaintance (he had known a number of home-grown communists during the 1930s and 1940s) gave him the "chill feeling" that

> while they might like me, or even love me, they could still kill me or destroy my reputation with no more than a sigh if this were "for the good of the party," or even if they thought it weren't but had been ordered to anyway. ... In this sense none of my group [of self-actualizing persons] is a fanatic. They are not killers of people "for the good of the people" or killers of good people "for the sake of advancing goodness." The others kill the individual for the sake of the rubric, the equation, the formula, the concept. ... These people get the world all classified and then live in their own stable, unchanging world of rubrics and don't even *see* flux, change, individuals.

Maslow did in fact "make much of" this characteristic, for in the paper of 1950 we find it broken up into at least four different headings: "freshness of appreciation," *"Gemeinschaftsgefühl"* (feeling of community, of brotherhood), "democratic character structure," and "philosophical, unhostile sense of humor."

Maslow's entries in the GHB notebook began to taper off in 1947. He had fallen ill toward the end of 1946, with a condition that was long afterward diagnosed as a heart attack. Early in 1947 he moved to California to recuperate, and there he remained until the middle of 1949. He continued making entries in the notebook from time to time, but these were mostly brief,

[11]A. H. Maslow, "Cognition of the Particular and the Generic," *Psychological Review,* 1948, **55**, 22–40.

factual, and unrevealing. We can only infer the course that his thoughts were following during this period from the distance between where they started and where they ended up.

"Self-Actualization:
A Study of Psychological Health"

Passing from Maslow's GHB notebook to his published paper of 1950 is like going from a diamond mine to Cartier's: one has the impression that somewhere along the way there has been a great deal of shaping, polishing, and setting. The vision of self-actualization that appeared in the notebook was groping and tentative, to say the least. True, most of the elements of the 1950 paper were there, but they were there only in the rough. In sharp contrast, the vision presented in the published paper was finely cut, polished, and set. Also, notwithstanding Maslow's apologies for methodological short-comings, it was presented with a confidence that could scarcely be described as groping or tentative. Maslow seems to have written the final version of the paper around the middle of 1949, just as he was returning from his recuperation in California. It would seem that the self-actualization concept achieved its definitive form for him at about this same time and that the preceding two years of illness and relative inactivity had served as a kind of incubation period.

From the very beginning, one of Maslow's greatest concerns about his self-actualization concept was that it might be seen by others as simply "some essence or Platonic idea which [does not] exist anywhere but in my own mind." His concern was well founded, for this indeed has been the criticism most often raised against the concept—that it was merely the prod-uct of his own mind, that it was nothing more than his own private notion of what constitutes an ideal person. The criticism has usually revolved around the methodological question of selection criteria. That is, on what basis had Maslow selected his potentially self-actualizing college students? On what basis had he selected his public and historical figures? Indeed, on what basis had he selected his "self-actualized adults over fifty or sixty" all along?

In his "Theory of Human Motivation" of 1943, Maslow had por-trayed self-actualization as a motivational state that tends to emerge when the more prepotent needs have been fairly well satisfied. In an unpublished note of the same year he indicated that this was precisely the criterion he was then using: "The point from which I start," he wrote, "is that [the self-actualizing person is one] whose basic needs have been more or less well satisfied, and then I have tried to dig up case histories of people who could fit into this category." By the time he started working with his students, however, he did not seem to have this criterion quite so explicitly before him. He seemed, instead, to be selecting persons whom he judged, "just by looking at them in class," to be nice, decent, good human beings.

Of course, Maslow had held all along that self-actualization was in some sense identical with psychological health. But psychological health, in the ordinary sense of the term, was never a criterion of selection—only of rejection. It was a necessary condition but not a sufficient one. In the introduction to his 1950 paper, Maslow indicated that his subjects had all been selected on the basis of one "negative criterion" and one "positive criterion." The negative criterion required that something be absent from his subjects —namely, "neurosis, psychopathic personality, psychosis, or strong tendencies in these directions." The positive criterion, on the other hand, required that something be present. That something was still "as yet a difficult syndrome to describe accurately, [though] it may be loosely described as the full use and exploitation of talents, capacities, potentialities, etc." It also required, or rather implied, "either gratification, past or present, of the basic emotional needs for safety, belongingness, love, respect, and self-respect, and of the cognitive needs for knowledge and for understanding, or, in a few cases, conquest of these needs."[12]

This was the fullest and most explicit statement of his selection criteria that Maslow ever gave. It did succeed in tying off two loose ends, but there was another left dangling. Thus Maslow indicated that he had used three criteria in selecting his subjects: (1) that they be free of psychopathology, (2) that their basic needs be gratified (or at least conquered), and (3) that they have fully actualized their potentialities. Now, the first two of these are subject in some degree to empirical determination: there are widely recognized ways of determining whether a person is free of manifest and even latent psychopathology; undoubtedly we could also agree on a set of objective means for determining whether, and to what degree, a person's basic needs have been gratified or overcome. The third criterion, however, is another thing entirely. The problem is this: how can we determine that a person has fully actualized his potentialities unless we know what his full potentialities are? Then again, how are we ever to know what his full potentialities are except by observing his actualities? (As Aristotle put it, potentiality is proved only by actuality.) Perhaps the difference between self-actualizing persons and ordinary mankind, then, is not that the former have more fully actualized their potentialities, but simply that they had greater potential to begin with. Let us also consider that there are many different kinds of human potentialities. For example, some persons have the potential to become mean bastards, and some of them actualize that potentiality very fully indeed. But would we be willing to say that these persons are, to that extent, self-actualized?

---

[12] *Motivation and Personality*, pp. 200–201.

We resort to these contrived alternatives only to point out that Maslow's third selection criterion was wrapped up in a rather large extra-empirical assumption. He had been guided throughout by a vision of human nature, and it was in the third criterion that the influence of this vision became most evident. Indeed, we could justly rephrase that criterion as follows: (3) that they have fully actualized those potentialities which *I take* to be most truly characteristic of human nature. We began by mentioning the view of some of Maslow's critics that "self-actualization" was simply his own private notion of what constitutes an ideal person. Maslow certainly would have been the first to admit that it *was* his own notion of "ideal person." Whether it was also private, in the sense of being merely a matter of taste or aesthetic preference, was of course quite another question—though we should not be surprised that it was raised.[13]

Selection criteria aside, let us go on to see what characteristics Maslow found in his self-actualizing persons. We shall not be following the exact order in which he listed these characteristics; also, since there was much overlap among them, we shall not be mentioning every characteristic separately.

Perception of, and Dealings with, Reality

As we mentioned earlier, the very first characteristic went under the heading "more efficient perception of reality and more comfortable relations with it." In a manner reminiscent of his statement of it in the GHB notebook, Maslow introduced this characteristic by saying that

> the first form in which this capacity was noticed was as an unusual ability to detect the spurious, the fake, and the dishonest in personality, and in general to judge people correctly and efficiently.... As the study progressed, it slowly became apparent that this efficiency extended to many other areas of life—indeed *all* areas that were tested. In art and music, in things of the intellect, in scientific matters, in politics and public affairs, they seemed as a group to be able to see concealed or confused realities more swiftly and more correctly than others.... At first this was phrased as good taste or good judgment. But for many reasons ..., it has become progressively more clear that this had better be called perception (not taste) of something that was absolutely there (reality, not a set of opinions).[14]

[13]In 1967 Maslow wrote in his Journal: "I meant to write and publish a self-actualization critique, but somehow never did. Now I think I know why. I think I had a hidden, unconscious criterion of selection *beyond* health. Why did I get so excited over Arthur E. Morgan, just from reading his book—so sure he was a self-actualizing person? It's because he was using the B-language! What I've done was to pick B-people! In addition to all the overt and conscious criteria. People in the B-realm using B-language, the awakened, the illuminated, the 'high plateau' people who normally B-cognize and who have the B-values very firmly and actively in hand." What Maslow meant by "B-language," "B-realm," and the like, should become clearer in the next chapter.

[14]*Motivation and Personality*, pp. 203–204.

Whether judgments in art, music, politics, and the like can ever be anything more than matters of taste, even for self-actualizing persons, is a very large question indeed. Maslow did not go on at this point to confront the question directly, though he did add a word about his hopes for confronting it later: "For those who have wrestled with this problem [of taste vs. reality], it will be clear that we may have here a partial basis for a true science of values, and consequently of ethics, social relations, politics, religion, etc." But more of that anon.

The principal reason why self-actualizing persons see reality more clearly is that they see it through an unclouded lens. They place no unrealistic, neurotic demands on reality; thus they distinguish

> far more easily than most the fresh, concrete, and idiographic from the generic, abstract, and rubricized. The consequence is that they live more in the real world of nature than in the man-made mass of concepts, abstractions, expectations, beliefs, and stereotypes that most people confuse with the world. They are therefore far more apt to perceive what is there rather than their own wishes, hopes, fears, anxieties, their own theories and beliefs, or those of their cultural group.

But it is not only that self-actualizing persons see the world as it really is; they also accept it as it really is. The result is that they are more comfortable with what they see and less fearful of what they do not see. Again, it is because they place no neurotic demands on reality:

> Our healthy subjects are uniformly unthreatened and unfrightened by the unknown, being therein quite different from average men. They accept it, are comfortable with it, and, often, are even *more* attracted by it than by the known. They not only tolerate the ambiguous and unstructured; they like it.

Being thus unthreatened by the unknown, self-actualizing persons are also happily free of superstitions: "They do not have to spend any time laying the ghost, whistling past the cemetery, or otherwise protecting themselves against imaginary dangers."[15]

The self-actualizing person's clearer perception and greater acceptance of reality have a great effect on his relationships with himself, with other persons, and with his society as a whole. Indeed, of the sixteen or so characteristics that Maslow listed, about half were chiefly concerned with the various aspects of human relationships. Thus the second characteristic that he mentioned had to do with the self-actualizing person's extraordinary acceptance of himself, of others, and of human nature. Because self-actualizing persons see reality more clearly, "they see human nature as it *is* and not

[15]*Motivation and Personality*, p. 206.

as they would prefer it to be." And just as they see and accept nonhuman nature as it is, so too do they see and accept human nature:

> One does not complain about water because it is wet, or about rocks because they are hard, or about trees because they are green. As the child looks out upon the world with wide, uncritical, innocent eyes, so does the self-actualizing person look upon human nature in himself and in others.

Thus self-actualizing persons do not suffer crippling shame, guilt, or anxiety over their own natures; neither do they despise the natures of others. The result is that they can enjoy life to the full. As Maslow put it, they tend to be

> good and lusty animals, hearty in their appetites and enjoying themselves mightily without regret or shame or apology. They seem to have a uniformly good appetite for food; they seem to sleep well; they seem to enjoy their sexual lives without unnecessary inhibition; and so on for all the relatively physiological impulses. They are able to [enjoy] themselves . . . at all [other] levels as well. . . . All of these are accepted without question as worthwhile, simply because these people are inclined to accept the work of nature rather than to argue with her for not having constructed things to a different pattern.

All of this, however, is not to say that the self-actualizing person is complacent and unambitious. He does at times feel discontent with human reality as he sees it in either himself or others. In fact, he may feel it very often and very intensely. Always, however, it is in accordance with a principle: "The general formula seems to be that healthy people will feel bad about discrepancies between what is and what might very well be or ought to be."[16]

Several other characteristics fall under this same heading and follow fairly directly from what has already been said. Thus we learn from Maslow that the self-actualizing person has a quality of detachment and a sense of privacy; that he is his own man, autonomous, relatively independent of his surroundings and highly "resistant to enculturation"; that he identifies with, and genuinely desires to help, all of humanity *(Gemeinschaftsgefühl);* that he prefers a few profound friendships to many superficial ones; that he is possessed of a "democratic character structure"; and that he has a philosophical, unhostile sense of humor. He loves others as he loves himself—in spite of shortcomings. Also, he is as unhostile and unaggressive toward others as toward himself; he intentionally hurts others only when it is "deserved . . . [or] for the good of the person attacked or for someone else's good." He is, in short, an altogether Good Human Being.

All in all, there is a striking resemblance between self-actualizing persons and those whom the prophet Micah described as "doing justly, loving

---

[16]*Motivation and Personality,* pp. 207–208.

mercy, and walking humbly with their God." Maslow was of course aware of the implication and quick to put it in its proper place:

> A few centuries ago these [self-actualizing persons] would all have been described as men who walk in the path of God or as Godly men. So far as religion is concerned, none of my subjects is orthodoxly religious, but on the other hand I know of only one who describes himself as an atheist. . . . The few others for whom I have information hesitate to call themselves atheists. They say they believe in a God, but describe this God more as a metaphysical concept than as a personal figure. . . . If religion is defined only in social-behavioral terms, then these are all religious people, the atheists included. But if more conservatively we use the term religion so as to include and stress the supernatural element and institutional orthodoxy . . ., our answer must be quite different, for then almost none of them is religious.[17]

There is another respect, too, in which Maslow's self-actualizers resemble the godly men of yore: almost all of them have had "the mystic experience."

Maslow recounted that his "interest and attention in this subject was first enlisted by several of my subjects who [their sense of privacy notwithstanding] described their sexual orgasms in vaguely familiar terms which later I remembered had been used by various writers to describe what *they* called the mystic experience." He then went on to characterize the experience in terms strongly reminiscent of the ones he had used in 1928:

> There were the same feelings of limitless horizons opening up to the vision, the feeling of being simultaneously more powerful and also more helpless than one ever was before, the feeling of great ecstasy and wonder and awe, the loss of placing in time and space with, finally, the conviction that something extremely important and valuable had happened, so that the subject is to some extent transformed and strengthened even in his daily life by such experiences.[18]

Of couse, sexual orgasm is not the only condition under which the mystic experience occurs. In fact, it would seem that any experience is a mystic one to the extent that there is "tremendous intensification" and "loss of self or transcendence of it." Everyone doubtless has such "mystic experiences" in greater or lesser degree and frequency; it is only that the self-actualizing person has them more often and more intensely. He is more open to reality and less threatened by it. Accordingly, he has

> the wonderful capacity to appreciate again and again, freshly and naïvely, the basic goods of life, with awe, pleasure, wonder, and even ecstasy, however stale these experiences may have become to others. Thus for such a person, any sunset may be as beautiful as the first one, any flower may be of breath-taking loveliness, even after he has seen a million flowers.[19]

[17] *Motivation and Personality*, p. 221.
[18] *Motivation and Personality*, p. 216.
[19] *Motivation and Personality*, pp. 214–215.

In the final reckoning, to say that the self-actualizing person has his full share of such "peak-experiences" is simply to say again that he sees reality more clearly; for the world is, after all, a place of great wonder and awesome beauty.

At any rate, this too put Maslow's self-actualizing persons in the realm of those who "walk with God." It is hardly surprising that his subjects sometimes drew "semireligious conclusions," such as "life must have a meaning," from their mystic experiences. It is also not surprising that this was as close as they ever came to a religious conclusion. As in his early paper on Emerson, Maslow observed that we must "dissociate this experience from any theological or supernatural reference, even though for thousands of years they have been linked. None of our subjects spontaneously made any such tie-up."[20] We shall consider Maslow's "peak-experiences" at greater length in the next chapter.

Spontaneity and Creativeness

Another characteristic that Maslow listed for self-actualizing persons was spontaneity. He was quick to point out, however, that he was not talking about mere eccentricity or—what is more common—pointed, ostentatious nonconformity. His notion was that the self-actualizing person is deeply and essentially spontaneous and nonconforming. This is not to say that he is unremittingly bizarre and unconventional. He can be altogether conventional if the occasion requires it, providing it does not conflict with his principles. The difference is that, whereas the ordinary person is conventional automatically, the self-actualizing person is so only voluntarily and by design. Thus, even though the self-actualizing person may forego acting on his impulses for the sake of conventionality (which is up to a point a valuable lubricant of human society), he is nonetheless aware of those impulses, accepting of them, and prepared to act on them should he consider it important to do so. This is the sense in which we may say that the self-actualizing person is deeply and essentially spontaneous, even when he might not seem to be so on the surface.

There is another respect, too, in which self-actualizing persons are spontaneous. It has to do with the "concept of motivation, [which perhaps] should apply only to non-self-actualizers." As Maslow put it:

> Our subjects no longer strive in the ordinary sense, but rather develop. They attempt to grow to perfection and to develop more and more fully in their own style. The motivation of ordinary men is a striving for the basic need gratifications that they lack. But self-actualizing people in fact lack none of these gratifications; and yet they have impulses. They work, they try, and

[20] *Motivation and Personality*, p. 216.

they are ambitious, even though in an unusual sense. For them motivation is just character growth, character expression, maturation, and development; in a word, self-actualization.[21]

He held, in short, that the behavior of ordinary mankind is under the *control* of what we might call deficiency-motivation, whereas that of self-actualizing persons is better described as an *expression,* an unfolding, of quite another kind of motivation (he later called it Being-motivation and meta-motivation). And here it was that Maslow returned to the question he had asked himself earlier, in the GHB notebook: "Could these self-actualizing people be more human, more revealing of the original nature of the species, closer to the species-type in the taxonomical sense? Ought a biological species to be judged by its crippled, warped, only partially developed specimens?" We have already seen his answer.

Because self-actualizing persons are motivated chiefly by the urge to become all that they are capable of being, and because, too, of their clearer perception of reality, they all show "in one way or another a special kind of creativeness or originality or inventiveness." Maslow is not speaking here of the "special-talent creativeness" of a Mozart or an Einstein, but rather of something that is "kin to the naïve and universal creativeness of unspoiled children." It is the kind of creativeness that seems to be "a fundamental characteristic of common human nature—a potentiality given to all human beings at birth," though lost by most as they become enculturated. Neither should it be imagined that the creativeness of the self-actualizing person extends only to such conventionally recognized forms as music, art, writing, and the like. Quite the contrary, his creativeness reaches out and touches everything that he does. It can even attach itself to such humble activities as scrubbing a floor or cooking a pot of canned soup. Indeed, the self-actualizing person's creativeness is not so much something he *does* as something he *is.* Were it not for the "choking-off forces" of enculturation and ungratified basic needs, "we might expect that every human being would show this special type of creativeness."[22]

Problem-Centering: Means and Ends,
Resolution of Dichotomies, Perception of Values

In 1946 Maslow published a well-received paper entitled "Problem-Centering vs. Means-Centering in Science,"[23] in which he argued that scientists—particularly psychologists—are sometimes so wrapped up in the task

[21] *Motivation and Personality,* p. 211.
[22] *Motivation and Personality,* pp. 223–224.
[23] A. H. Maslow, "Problem-Centering vs. Means-Centering in Science," *Philosophy of Science,* 1946, **13**, 326–331.

of refining their research methods that they lose sight of the problems for which those methods were originally intended. He described the most extreme form of this phenomenon as "methodolatry," the mindless worship of methodology and the inability to see that it is but a means to a higher end. In the 1950 paper this same methodolatry, or rather its absence, appeared as a characteristic of the self-actualizing person. Maslow considered the self-actualizing person to be "problem-centered" in two senses. The first is that, because he sees reality clearly, he suffers no confusion between ends and means, problems and methods; in this sense he is problem-centered rather than "means-centered." The second sense is that he is problem-centered rather than "ego-centered." This again is because he sees reality clearly, though here we are speaking more specifically of the fact that the self-actualizing person's vision is unclouded by the cataract of deficiency-motivation. Thus he sees the problem and its possible solutions as they *are* rather than as he or others might like them to be.

An important result of the latter is that the self-actualizing person perceives many "problems" to be merely pseudoproblems. The ordinary man tends to dichotomize reality, to categorize and rubricize it, to partition it into discrete, mutually exclusive parcels; and many of the issues that the ordinary man considers to be problematical inhere not so much in reality itself as in this ego-centered process by which he systematically distorts reality. For the self-actualizing person, on the other hand, all such false dichotomies are resolved, "the polarities disappear, and many oppositions thought to be intrinsic merge and coalesce with each other to form unities." Maslow listed the following, among others, as examples of such false dichotomies: reason-emotion, kindness-ruthlessness, concreteness-abstractness, acceptance-rebellion, self-society, serious-humorous, conventional-unconventional, mystic-realistic (!), active-passive, masculine-feminine, Eros-Agape.[24]

What this resolution of false dichotomies means in practice is that, for the self-actualizing person, "conflict and struggle, ambivalence and uncertainty over choice lessen or disappear in many areas of life." And not the least of these areas is the realm of morals, ethics, and values, wherein the self-actualizing person perceives many of the "problems" to be merely "the gratuitous epiphenomena of the pervasive psychopathology of the average" —merely misbegotten, "sick-man-created" trivialities. Thus the self-actualizing person is not likely to be found anguishing over such pseudoproblems as "exposing the head (in some churches) or not exposing the head (in others), . . . eating some meats and not others, or eating them on some days but not on others, . . . relations between the sexes, attitudes toward the structure of the body and toward its functioning, and toward death itself." For him all such "problems" melt away in the heat of "pagan acceptance."[25]

[24] *Motivation and Personality*, p. 233.
[25] *Motivation and Personality*, pp. 230–231.

Even in those cases in which the self-actualizing person does find a question of ethics or values to be genuine, we shall not find him anguishing over it. This is not because he is callous, but because for him there is simply no conflict or ambiguity in such matters. He is "automatically furnished" at every turn with "a firm foundation for a value system." We have already encountered the frame of this foundation under the heading of spontaneity: it is the self-actualizing person's own ingenuous, healthy impulses, which he accepts and trusts—as well he should, for they are all directed to the high ends of character growth, character expression, maturation, and development. So, once again, the self-actualizing person resembles the godly man of old. As Maslow put it, "St. Augustine's 'Love God and do as you will' can easily be translated, 'Be healthy and then you may trust your impulses.' "[26]

Imperfections

Maslow believed that his self-actualizing persons stood about as close to perfection as it is possible for a human being to be, but he did not consider that they had reached perfection entirely. Even in later years he was never fully convinced that it is possible to achieve complete self-actualization —complete human perfection—within the brief span of a single lifetime. Indeed, he seemed at times to find this residual imperfection rather comforting, as though it were a sign that the self-actualizing person, in spite of his great progress toward perfection, is really human after all. As early as 1943, in the unpublished note cited earlier, he observed that "people who are not themselves healthy are apt to have a highly contorted view of what the healthy person is like, are apt to make him quite unreal and not entirely human. It is necessary therefore to stress the human weaknesses and small feelings, the feet of clay of the person who is healthy." In the 1950 paper he noted similarly that the self-actualizing person must not be made to seem "so good that he is a caricature, so that nobody would like to be like him. . . . Most of [those] who have attempted to portray good (healthy) people did this sort of thing, making them into stuffed shirts or marionettes or unreal projections of unreal ideals, rather than into the robust, healthy, lusty individuals they really are." This is a great error, for self-actualizing (good, healthy) people do in fact show

> many of the lesser human failings. They too are equipped with silly, waste-
> ful, or thoughtless habits. They can be boring, stubborn, irritating. They are
> by no means free from a rather superficial vanity, pride, partiality to their
> own productions, family, friends, and children. Temper outbursts are not
> rare.

[26] *Motivation and Personality*, pp. 230–233.

Furthermore, the self-actualizing person is not entirely free of guilt, anxiety, sadness, self-castigation, internal strife, and conflict (though in his case these do not arise from neurotic sources). Also, his tendency to find all experience full of wonder, beauty, and fascination sometimes leads him to seem absent-minded or humorless and to forget the conventional social amenities. Then, too, he sometimes gets into trouble because of his loving kindness, which may lead him into such mistakes as "marrying out of pity, getting too closely involved with neurotics, bores, unhappy people, and then being sorry for it, allowing scoundrels to impose on him for a while, giving more than he should so that occasionally he encourages parasites and psychopaths, etc." Finally, there is a shortcoming of self-actualizing persons that cannot be counted among these "lesser human failings." It is that they can sometimes show an extraordinary and abrupt ruthlessness. Even this, though, can be forgiven, for it happens only in the service of a higher justice: "It must be remembered that they are very strong people. This makes it possible for them to display a surgical coldness when this is called for, beyond the power of the average man."[27]

Yes, it is easy to forgive the self-actualizing person his "faults," for he is on balance a very fine creature indeed. Who, in truth, would not "like to be like him"? Whatever else it might have been, Maslow's "self-actualization" was a modern-day vision not just of human health, but of beatitude. It was, of course, thoroughly clad in the secular garments of psychology (albeit not in the official dress uniform), but it was a vision of beatitude nonetheless. It was doubtless this that accounted for much of the widespread enthusiasm generated by the notion of self-actualization both within psychology and without. Perhaps there are those who can endure life without such a vision, but there are at least equally many who would rather not. And many of the latter find scant comfort in the traditional, religious visions, for they have all heard Zarathustra's message—with which Maslow devoutly agreed—that God is dead. Nietzsche had his Zarathustra proclaim: "God is dead, and now I teach you the Overman." Maslow's proclamation had much the same prophetic tone: ". . . and now I teach you self-actualization." Of course, we ought not make too much of such similarities; but neither ought we make too little of them.

We still have before us the question of whether "self-actualization" is *true.* The answer that we eventually give must depend in large measure on what we understand the question to mean. Are there persons in this world who have (in varying degrees and combinations) the empirical characteristics that Maslow described? Certainly our answer to this would be a qualified yes. Is there presently research evidence in psychology to support the hypothesis that these characteristics are significantly associated with psychological

[27] *Motivation and Personality,* pp. 228–229.

health? In my opinion the answer is: yes, some, though it is hardly overwhelming. (It must be said in fairness that psychology does not abound in
hypotheses for which the evidence is overwhelming, except in a few special-
ized areas such as physiological psychology, sensation and perception, and
simple animal learning.) Finally, is the self-actualizing person the truest rep-
resentation of what human nature really *is* beneath the surface? This, of
course, is one of those very large questions to which only fools and visionaries
dare offer definitive answers. Maslow was certainly no fool, but a visionary
he was most assuredly. In this respect at least, he was the brother of the
psychoanalyst, the behaviorist, and the proponent of every other psychological "ism," for what he offered in "self-actualization" was not just a psychological fact but a full-blown vision of human nature. His vision, however, was
unique. Where all the others dwelt on eroticism or power or self-integration
or stimulus and response, Maslow's was a vision of gnostic truth and pagan
joy. We can do no better than to close this chapter as we began, with the
words of Friedrich Nietzsche:

> *O Mensch! Gib acht!*
> *Was spricht die tiefe Mitternacht?*
> *Ich schlief, ich schlief—*
> *Aus tiefem Traum bin ich erwacht:*
> *Die Welt ist tief,*
> *Und tiefer als der Tag gedacht.*
> *Tief ist ihr Weh—*
> *Lust—tiefer noch als Herzeleid:*
> *Weh spricht: Vergeh!*
> *Doch alle Lust will Ewigkeit—*
> *—will tiefe, tiefe Ewigkeit!*

> (O Man, give heed!
> What does the deep of night declare?
> I was sleeping, sleeping—
> From a deep dream I awoke:
> The world is deep,
> Far deeper than the day had thought.
> Deep is its woe, its anguish—
> But deeper yet its joy:
> Woe says: Be gone!
> But all joy wills eternity—
> Wills deep, deep eternity!)

4

Peak-Experience

A Tzaddik stood at the window in the early morning light and, trembling, cried, "A few hours ago it was night and now it is day—God brings up the day!" And he was full of fear and trembling. He also said, "Every creature should be ashamed before the Creator: were he perfect, as he was destined to be, then he would be astonished and awakened and inflamed because of the renewal of Creation at each time and in each moment."—Martin Buber, "The Life of the Chassidim," 1908.

"I am well aware," wrote William James as he concluded his great classic *Varieties of Religious Experience*, "that after all the palpitating documents I have quoted, . . . the dry analysis to which I now advance may appear to many of you like an anti-climax, a tapering-off and flattening-out of the subject, instead of a crescendo of interest and result." We must begin this chapter with a similar admission. There is really no way of succinctly conveying the richness, the spirit, the *je ne sais quoi*, of Maslow's writings on the subject of peak-experience. The best we can do is convey the gist of what he had to say—and that by way of a rather "dry analysis." The result, to those who are directly acquainted with Maslow's words on the subject, will certainly seem pale and lifeless by comparison. It is unfortunate but unavoidable. In any event, there will be no risk of misunderstanding as long as the reader bears in mind that what he is being given is only a menu, not the meal itself.

Maslow began presenting his views on peak-experience in about 1956, but they reached their largest audience only with the publication in

1962 of his book *Toward a Psychology of Being.*[1] The title of the book itself
is a good indication of the course Maslow's thoughts had followed during the
preceding decade. In his work on self-actualization he had sought to go
beyond normal psychology to a truer vision of human nature. Now, with his
studies of peak-experience, he was seeking to go beyond human nature to a
truer vision of reality at large.

    This should not come entirely as a surprise, for every vision of human
nature is in some degree a vision of reality at large—and Maslow's was more
so than most. In the preceding chapter we dwelt at length on his notion that
the self-actualizing person sees reality more clearly. Now we must ask the
obvious question: how could Maslow tell? How could he judge that his
subjects saw reality more clearly unless he already had before him a vision
of what reality really is? The question is even more obvious when we come
to consider Maslow's work on peak-experience. His first and principal paper
on this subject was significantly entitled "Cognition of Being in the Peak-
Experiences."[2] The title expressed his belief that the peak-experience is not
merely a mood or a state of mind, but a genuine revelation of reality. Moreover, he held it to be a revelation not just of mundane, ordinary reality, but
of whatever it is that lies hidden behind the veil—in short, of Being itself.
Again the question is: how could he tell? How could he judge that the
peak-experience amounts to a "cognition of Being" unless he already had an
inkling of what Being truly is? The answer, of course, is that he could not.
Maslow's psychology, like that of John Locke three centuries earlier, consisted in part of "a little excursion into natural philosophy."

    By way of analogy, imagine a world in which the average person is
color-blind. Imagine further that a psychologist in that world believes or
suspects that the familiar black, white, and gray objects of ordinary visual
experience are in reality possessed of a marvelous and variegated property
that he calls "hue." Perhaps at times, in extraordinary moments, he has even
seen these hues himself. If, now, he could find other persons who also see the
world (at least at times) in its true colors, his case would be all the stronger.
If he could demonstrate that these color-sighted persons are in fact healthier
than the color-blind, and that the latter have only a degenerate, crippled form
of vision, his case would be stronger still.

    The analogy is a fair one, for we must recall that Maslow was no
stranger to revelation of the sort that he described. "I have myself had the
mystic experience," he had written in 1928, and in that very moment it was
revealed to him that mankind holds "wonderful possibilities and inscrutable
depths." Then later, when the concept of self-actualization came upon him,
it did not come lumberingly on foot, but on wings, in one wonderfully

[1] A. H. Maslow, *Toward a Psychology of Being* (New York: Van Nostrand, 1962).
[2] A. H. Maslow, "Cognition of Being in the Peak-Experiences." *Journal of Genetic Psychology,* 1959, **94,** 43–66.

exciting moment of realization. These are but two examples; even the most cursory examination of Maslow's published and private writings will indicate that he was well acquainted, at first hand, with experiences of the kind that he called "peak." "I had lots of them," he once wrote in his journals. "I remember. I think I used to call it 'exultation' to myself, with lump in throat, tears in eyes, chills, prickles, slight feeling of (pleasant) nausea, and all sorts of other autonomic reactions plus impulse to shout and yell, etc."[3] We noted earlier that Maslow's interest in self-actualization did not arise in a vacuum; neither, we must add, did his interest in peak-experience.

Maslow described his paper on peak-experience as "an attempt to generalize in a single description some of the basic cognitive happenings in the B-love experience, the parental experience, the mystic, or oceanic, or nature experience, the aesthetic perception, the creative moment, the therapeutic or intellectual insight, the orgasmic experience, certain forms of athletic fulfillment, etc." As with the paper on self-actualization, this one was presented not as a formal research report but as an "impressionistic, ideal, 'composite photograph.'" It was the result, Maslow wrote, of interviews with about eighty persons and of written responses by 190 college students to the following instructions:

> I would like you to think of the most wonderful experience or experiences of your life: happiest moments, ecstatic moments, moments of rapture, perhaps from being in love, or from listening to music or suddenly "being hit" by a book or a painting, or from some great creative moment. First list these. And then try to tell me how you feel in such acute moments, how you feel *differently* from the way you feel at other times, how you are at the moment a different person in some ways. (With [some] subjects the question asked rather about the ways in which the world looked different.)[4]

Maslow indicated that his data also included about fifty unsolicited descriptions of peak-experiences from persons who had read of his interest in the subject; in addition, he had "tapped the immense literatures of mysticism, religion, art, creativeness, love, etc."

It is important to note that no single one of Maslow's subjects reported the full syndrome that he went on to describe. This full syndrome was rather his own creation, in much the same way that a character portrait is the creation of the artist who draws it. As Maslow put it: "I have added together all the partial responses [of individual subjects] to make a 'perfect' composite syndrome." It perhaps goes without saying that a creative process of this sort is not so much one of "adding together" as it is of selecting, sharpening, emphasizing, ordering, and interpreting. Much the same can be said of that other well-known psychological study of extraordinary states of mind, James'

[3]Journal entry, November 1964.
[4]*Psychology of Being*, p. 67.

Varieties. James, too, sought to draw a kind of composite picture of what he in his own day was pleased to call religious experience. He, too, had to pass his data through the creative forge of selecting, sharpening, emphasizing, and so forth. Finally, as we shall see in a moment, he, too, already had an inkling of what that reality, to which all such experiences allude, really is. We shall have more to say on this subject toward the end of the chapter.

There is another respect, too, in which James' and Maslow's treatments of the subject may be compared. James wrote leisurely and at length and never made a point without presenting the reader with a sample of the "raw data"—that is, without presenting an extended first-person account of the experiences in question. Maslow seemed to be in more of a hurry, and it is the unfortunate irony of his writings on peak-experience that they did not follow their own precept. Not the least property of the experience, as Maslow portrayed it, is that it is direct and concrete rather than abstract and generalized. And yet, in describing the experience, what he mainly gave were abstract generalizations; rarely did he offer a concrete illustration of the sort that James gave at every turn. Of course, life is short, and there is only so much that one man can do. Certainly Maslow felt this more sharply than most—that he had much to do and precious little time to do it in. Then, too, there is the fact that he had a keen sense of privacy about such matters. In his journals he recorded that in his earlier years he always kept his own peak-experiences to himself—"absolutely secret." Even as late as 1964 he wrote: "I *still* find myself somewhat embarrassed to talk about my own experiences and rarely do." He seemed curiously reluctant to confide his peak-experiences even to his own private journals; these contain a great many mentions of his peak-experiences but almost nothing in the way of *description.* At any rate, it is fair to say that Maslow has provided us with a large-scale topographic map of the area as he saw it, but with few fine-grain surface details.

Let us, then, proceed exactly as Maslow did, by presenting "in a condensed summary the characteristics of the cognition found in the generalized peak-experience." We shall find it convenient to discuss these characteristics under three headings: (1) the properties of the experience itself, (2) what the experience proclaims—what it seems to reveal—about reality at large, and (3) its effects on the experiencer. It must of course be understood that there is much overlap and interconnection among these three realms.

Properties of the Experience

As we saw in the preceding chapter, a precondition for self-actualization is that the person's basic needs have been either gratified or overcome.

Another way of saying this is that the person must no longer be under the control of D(=deficiency)-motivation. Inasmuch as peak-experience is intimately related to self-actualization, it will come as no surprise that this is a precondition here as well.

Indeed, Maslow often used the phrases "peak-experience" and "B-cognition" (where B=Being, the opposite of deficiency) interchangeably. Thus the very first thing that he mentioned as a characteristic of peak-experience was also something of a definition: "In B-cognition the experience or the object [experienced] tends to be seen as ... detached from relations, from possible usefulness, from expediency, and from purpose. ... This contrasts with D-cognition, which includes most human cognitive experiences." The theme is of course a familiar one:

> Self-actualizing people are more able to perceive the world as if it were independent not only of them, but also of human beings in general. This also tends to be true of the average human being in his highest moments, i.e., in his peak-experiences. He can then more readily look upon nature as if it were there in itself and for itself, and not simply as if it were a playground put there for human purposes. He can more easily refrain from projecting human purposes upon it. In a word, he can see it in its own Being ... rather than as something to be used, or something to be afraid of, or to be reacted to in some other human way.[5]

Maslow was not one to beat around the bush; he let the reader know what he was about at the very outset. Just as the self-actualizing person sees reality more clearly as a matter of course, so too does the ordinary person see it more clearly in his peak-experiences. The peak-experience is not just a peculiar state of mind; it is a revelation of Being itself, of the Kantian *Ding an sich*. But more of this later.

Because the thing (or event, quality, person, and so on) experienced in the peak-experience is seen in and for itself, detached from relations, usefulness, expediency, and so forth, it is seen "as a whole, as a complete unit." Indeed, it is seen "as if it were all there was in the universe, as if it were all of Being, synonymous with the universe." It is accordingly attended to with complete absorption. Furthermore, since the thing experienced is for the time being "isolated from all else, as if the world were forgotten," it is seen individually and concretely rather than generically and abstractly. It is not compared or evaluated or judged—it is simply beheld. In this sense the peak-experience may be said to be passive and receptive rather than active. But though it is passive, it is not inert. As Maslow put it, "concrete perceiving of the whole of the object implies that it is seen with 'care,' " which is to say with love. He was of course referring not to the self-serving "love" that stems from D-motivation, but to that selfless B-love so characteristic of the self-

[5] *Psychology of Being,* pp. 70–72.

actualizing person. Among ordinary persons it is the kind of love that is best exemplified by "the caring minuteness with which a mother will gaze upon her infant again and again, or the lover at his beloved, or the connoisseur at his painting."[6]

The last characteristic that we may mention under this heading is that

> the peak-experience is felt as a self-validating, self-justifying moment which carries its own intrinsic value with it. . . . The peak-experience is only good and desirable, and is never experienced as evil or undesirable. The experience is intrinsically valid; the experience is perfect, complete, and needs nothing else. It is sufficient to itself. It is felt as being intrinsically necessary and inevitable. It is just as good as it *should* be.[7]

It is fair to point out that this particular characteristic of the peak-experience was partly guaranteed by the instructions that Maslow gave his subjects at the outset: "I would like you to think of the most wonderful . . . experiences of your life: happiest moments, ecstatic moments," and so on. His results might have been quite different had he asked his subjects to report the most intense and overwhelming experiences of their lives—without specifying "wonderful," "happy," and "ecstatic." As we shall see in a moment, the point bears strongly on what Maslow considered the peak-experience to proclaim about reality at large.

What the Experience Proclaims

James noted in his *Varieties* that, even though the mystical experience seems to him who has it to be a revelation of reality, its import remains essentially ineffable. Thus the cognitive content of the revelation can never be fully or accurately described but only hinted at. Maslow found the same characteristic in peak-experience. It is something like a color-sighted person's trying to describe his experience of the color yellow. There will be no difficulty if the person to whom he is speaking is himself color-sighted, for though the experience of yellow may be every bit as ineffable as the mystic or peak-experience, the one will know immediately, from his own experience, what the other is talking about. If the hearer has never himself experienced color, however, he will not gain the least idea of what yellow is like. Maslow was not overwhelmed by the problem, for he considered that almost everyone is color-sighted in at least some degree. That is, he believed that almost everyone has peak-experiences, mild and infrequent though they may be in the case of those who are not self-actualizing. Thus he had reason to hope

[6] *Psychology of Being,* pp. 70–72.
[7] *Psychology of Being,* pp. 74–76.

that the cognitive proclamation of the experience might be recognizable, at least dimly, to all.

The chief proclamation of the peak-experience is much the same as James described when he wrote of his own "mystical experiences," which were artificially induced by nitrous oxide. They all converged, he wrote,

> towards a kind of insight to which I cannot help ascribing some metaphysical significance. The keynote of it is invariably a reconciliation. It is as if the opposites of the world, whose contradictoriness and conflict make all our difficulties and troubles, were melted into unity. Not only do they, as contrasted species, belong to one and the same genus, but one of the species, the nobler and better one, is itself the genus, and so soaks up and absorbs its opposite into itself.[8]

James was cautious of expanding this "dark saying" into a universal truth; still, he admitted that he could not "wholly escape from its authority."

Neither could Maslow. He had already seen that, in the self-actualizing person, "many dichotomies, polarities, and conflicts are fused, transcended, or resolved." Thus what the ordinary person takes to be "straight-line continua, whose extremes are polar to each other and as far apart as possible," become for the self-actualizing person "rather like circles or spirals, in which the polar extremes come together into a fused unity." He found the same tendency toward "full cognition" in the peak-experiences of even quite ordinary persons. Here, then, as Maslow saw it, is the principal proclamation of the peak-experience: "The more we understand the whole of Being, the more we can tolerate the simultaneous existence and perception of inconsistencies, of oppositions, and of flat contradictions," for all of these are but "products of partial cognition and fade away with cognition of the whole."[9] In the true world, the world of Being revealed through the peak-experience, all seeming contrarieties are ultimately reconciled.

But these oppositions are not just reconciled—they are reconciled for good, rather than for ill. We have already met with Maslow's assertion that "the peak-experience is only good and desirable, and is never experienced as evil or undesirable." It was this declared characteristic of the experience that he had in mind when he observed:

> The philosophical implications here are tremendous. If . . . we accept the thesis that in peak-experience the nature of reality itself *may* be seen more clearly and its essence penetrated more profoundly, then this is almost the same as saying what so many philosophers and theologians have affirmed, that the whole of Being is only neutral or good, and that evil or pain or threat is only a partial phenomenon, a product of not seeing the world whole and unified, and of seeing it from a self-centered point of view.[10]

[8]William James, *The Varieties of Religious Experience* (New York: Longmans, Green and Co., 1902), p. 388.
[9]*Psychology of Being,* p. 86.
[10]*Psychology of Being,* pp. 76-77.

Maslow was not suggesting that the "whole of Being" is all beer and skittles. The goodness that he spoke of is not what the ordinary man would see as good but rather what Being itself proclaims as good. There is, in the peak-experience, a perception of values. These, however, are not the deficiency-motivated D-values that we ordinarily project on the world. Rather, they are the values—the B-values—of Being itself; they are "its values rather than our own."[11] As far as Maslow could "make out at this point," these values included such qualities as the following: wholeness, perfection, completion, justice ("oughtness"), aliveness, richness (differentiation, complexity, intricacy), simplicity, beauty, goodness, uniqueness (individuality, novelty), effortlessness (ease, grace, lack of strain, striving, or difficulty), playfulness (joy), truth, self-sufficiency. Let us repeat for emphasis that these values perceived in the peak-experience are not mere human projections. They transcend man in quite the same way that Being itself transcends man, for that is precisely where they inhere—in Being itself. Maslow certainly recognized that the point would remain obscure to anyone who had not himself experienced B-cognition.

In any event, the peak-experience seems to him who has it to be a revelation of reality. Considering the vastness, the wholeness, and the goodness of the reality thus revealed, we shall not be surprised to learn that the experience carries with it "a special flavor of wonder, of awe, of reverence, of humility and surrender before the experience as before something great" and that it infuses one with a "profound sense of humility, smallness, unworthiness before the enormity of the experience."[12] This, however, is only one side of it. The other side is best compared

> with one aspect of the concept of "god". . . . The gods who can contemplate the whole of Being, and who therefore understand it, must see it as good, just, inevitable, and must see "evil" as a product of limited or selfish vision and understanding. If we could be godlike in this sense, then we, too, out of universal understanding, would never blame or condemn or be disappointed or shocked. Our only possible emotions would be pity, charity, kindliness, and perhaps sadness or B-amusement with the shortcomings of the other. But this is precisely the way in which self-actualizing people do at times react to the world, and in which *all* of us react in our peak moments.[13]

In the preceding chapter we saw the resemblance between self-actualizing persons and the godly men of former ages; now we see that they resemble the *gods* of former ages too. And so do quite ordinary persons—in their peak moments.

[11] *Psychology of Being,* p. 78.
[12] *Psychology of Being,* pp. 82-83.
[13] *Psychology of Being,* p. 77.

Effects on the Experiencer

We shall return in a moment to the question of the cognitive validity of the peak-experience. First, however, we must examine the effects of the experience on the person who has it. Actually, the two are not unrelated. It was William James who put the argument most succinctly: if an experience brings one "inner happiness" and "good consequential fruits for life," these characteristics should not be left altogether out of account when we undertake to judge its cognitive validity. This of course does not mean that "the most wonderful experience of your life" is *ipso facto* true, for certainly "inner happiness" and truth are not inseparable. As James put it:

> What immediately feels most "good" is not always most "true" when measured by the verdict of the rest of experience. The difference between Philip drunk and Philip sober is the classic instance in corroboration. If merely "feeling good" could decide, drunkenness would be the supremely valid human experience. But its revelations, however acutely satisfying at the moment, are inserted into an environment which refuses to bear them out for any length of time.[14]

This, in fact, was the central question for James: does the rest of life and experience bear the revelation out? Do the experiences conduce, consistently and in the long run, to good living? If so, then we are provided, if not with a proof of their cognitive validity, at least with a presumption of it. Maslow did not put the argument quite so explicitly, but it was there all the same.

What, then, are these good and consequential fruits for life that are associated with the peak-experience? The largest and ripest falls from the branch that we have already mentioned: just as the peak-experience reveals the wholeness and goodness of the world outside the person, so too does it help to actualize the wholeness and goodness that lies latent within him. Thus we find in the experience "a fusion of ego, id, super-ego, and ego-ideal, of conscious and unconscious, of primary and secondary processes, a synthesizing of pleasure principle with reality principle, a regression without fear in the service of the greatest maturity, a true integration of the person at *all* levels."[15]

Of course, this conciliation of opposites within the personality lasts in its full form only as long as the peak-experience lasts. There are, however, several aftereffects that are more enduring. Certainly the foremost of these is that the peak-experience "can change more or less permanently [the person's] view of the world, or of aspects or parts of it." By the same token, it

[14] *Varieties of Religious Experience,* p. 422.
[15] *Psychology of Being,* p. 91.

can change his view of himself "in a healthy direction," as well as his view of other people and his behavior toward them. Then, too, the peak-experience can have actual psychotherapeutic effects; that is, it can cause the remission of neurotic symptoms. Finally, it can have the effect of "releasing" the person "for greater creativity, spontaneity, expressiveness, idiosyncracy"—in a word, for greater self-actualization. Thus, all in all, the person who has had the peak-experience "is more apt to feel that life in general is worthwhile, even if it is usually drab, pedestrian, painful, or ungratifying, since beauty, excitement, honesty, play, goodness, truth, and meaningfulness have been demonstrated to him to exist." Small wonder, then, that he "remembers the experience as a very important and desirable happening and seeks to repeat it." For what indeed is the peak-experience but "a visit to a personally defined Heaven from which the person then returns to earth"? Maslow fittingly concluded his observations on the aftereffects of peak-experience with a quotation from Coleridge:

> If a man could pass through Paradise in a dream, and have a flower presented to him as a pledge that his soul had really been there, and if he found that flower in his hand when he awoke—Ay! and what then?[16]

And what then indeed? Maslow devoted several pages of his paper to the question of the cognitive validity of the peak-experience—as well he might, for there certainly is one! He readily admitted that "just because the person *believes* that he perceives more truly and more wholly is no proof that he actually does so"; he also admitted that "the cognitive experiences I have been describing cannot be a substitute for the routine skeptical and cautious procedures of science." All the same, the overall tone of the paper left little room for doubt about where he stood; he believed the peak-experience to be often, if not always, a genuine revelation of Being. Otherwise, we should have to regard his interest in possibilities such as the following to be merely academic (and it should be clear by this time that Maslow's interests were never merely academic):

> If self-actualizing people can and do perceive reality more efficiently, fully, and with less motivational contamination than we others do, then we may possibly use them as biological assays. Through *their* greater sensitivity and perception, we may get a better report of what reality is like, than through our own eyes, just as canaries can be used to detect gas in mines before less sensitive creatures can. As a second string to this same bow, we may use ourselves in our most perceptive moments, in our peak-experiences, when, for the moment, *we* are self-actualizing, to give us a report of the nature of reality that is truer than we can ordinarily manage.[17]

[16] *Psychology of Being,* p. 95.
[17] *Psychology of Being,* p. 94.

We shall see later that Maslow followed this same line of thought when he undertook to deliver what he had promised earlier—"a true science of values, and consequently of ethics, social relations, politics, religion, etc."

If self-actualizing persons see reality more clearly as a matter of course, and *if* ordinary persons see it more clearly in their occasional peak-experiences (which are, after all, but acute episodes of self-actualization), then certainly we do have the makings for a cognitive expedition into the heartland of reality. But the question is: do they? Is the peak-experience truly a revelation of reality? For all we know, it is; but, then again, for all we know, it may simply be a happy diversion *from* reality. The fact is that Maslow has given us only two reasons to consider the former rather than the latter: first, that peak-experiences are always good and desirable and that they have salubrious aftereffects; second, that they are more closely associated with psychological health than with psychological unhealth. These reasons may permit us to entertain the cognitive validity of the peak-experience as a possibility, but they certainly do not oblige us to see it as a probability.

Let us nonetheless assume for the sake of discussion that the peak-experience is a genuine revelation of reality. Even with this there remains a very large and difficult question—namely, when it comes time to describe and interpret this essentially ineffable experience, to what extent is its cognitive import squeezed into the mold of the experiencer's own preconceptions? Maslow of course argued that the peak-experience is free of deficiency-motivated preconception, but this too is a hypothesis that is yet unproved. Besides, even if the experience itself is free of cognitive bias, it is by no means clear that the interpretation framed in its afterglow should be similarly free. James observed of the mystical experience that it is "capable of forming matrimonial alliances with materials furnished by the most diverse philosophies and theologies." Thus the mystical revelations of the medieval Christian tend to get interpreted in a manner consistent with trinitarian monotheism, those of the pantheist take on the cast of pantheism, and so on for the absolute idealist, the nature mystic, and all the rest. We are given no reason to suppose that things would be any different for the "peak" experience, save in that hypothetical case in which the person is so fully self-actualized that he is altogether innocent of preconceptions. I confess that I have never yet met such a person.

Finally, there is the question of the extent to which Maslow's interpretation of what the peak-experience reveals about Being might have been squeezed into the mold of *his* own preconceptions. He remarked at one point in his paper that "the exploration of the highest reaches of human nature and of its ultimate possibilities . . . has involved for me the continuous destruction of cherished axioms."[18] This, however, was surely intended as didactic

---

[18] *Psychology of Being,* p. 67.

hyperbole, for we have seen already that Maslow's explorations more often had the effect of confirming and extending his prior convictions. Perhaps he was surprised at many turns by what he found in his explorations of self-actualization and peak-experience, but it is unlikely that he was ever shocked or dismayed. His surprise was more akin to that of the shy lover who finds —*mirabile dictu!*—that his beloved loves him in return. That is, it was a surprise most pleasant and agreeable. The short of it is that Maslow did set out on his road with a compelling vision of what lay ahead, and that this vision did have a way of getting confirmed. And here, of course, is the great danger, for anyone who has a compelling vision of reality can always, if he tries hard enough, find data to support it. One is reminded of the Yiddish proverb *Az men vil a hunt a zets geben, gefint men a shteken* ("If you're out to beat a dog, you're sure to find a stick").

Let us take but one of the many available examples. In an undergraduate philosophy paper that seems to date from 1929 or 1930, Maslow wrote:

> The most superficial observation of facts serves to impress upon me overwhelmingly that we are not at home here [in the world]. . . . We are strangers, we are guests . . . [Some persons believe] that the world was made for us. I should rather say that we were made for the world. . . . To consider only mankind is fallacious. Mankind, it must be clearly borne in mind, is a result of the existence of the world, not its cause.

The world, he went on to argue, must be seen in itself, as it really is, not as we would like it to be; for only then shall we "succeed in banishing . . . the sense of impotence, of futility, of overbearing inimical power [directed against us] that we get when we turn our thoughts to the universe at large." We shall see that the universe is neither for us nor against us, that it is altogether impersonally "oblivious to our needs, our desires, and our hopes." It is only when we see things otherwise that we suffer from a "sense of the opposition, of the contrariety, and of the antagonism of the world." If only we could step outside of our self-centered point of view, we would find all this opposition, contrariety, and antagonism resolved.

Certainly Maslow's view of the "universe at large" evolved a great deal in the following decades. All the same, the theme of the undergraduate philosophy paper is clearly recognizable throughout much of his later writings, and especially in the following passage from the peak-experience paper. One answer to the "problem of evil," he wrote,

> is suggested by the way in which our subjects "accept reality" as being-in-itself, in its own right. It is neither *for* man nor is it *against* him. It is just impersonally what it is. An earthquake which kills poses a problem of reconciliation only for the man who needs a personal God. . . . For the man who can perceive it and accept it naturalistically, impersonally and as un-

created, it presents no ethical or axiological problem, since it wasn't done "on purpose" to annoy him.[19]

Of course, connections and confirmations of this sort do not mean that Maslow's prior expectations created his data out of nothingness, but they do leave open the possibility that the expectations refashioned the data somewhat in their own image.

All that we have just said may be summarized very briefly: Maslow's case in regard to the "cognition of Being" in the peak-experience is simply unproved; moreover, it is faced with difficult questions at every turn. We must hasten to add that Maslow was fully aware of all this and that he remained, as ever in the face of "insurmountable difficulties," undaunted. No man who traffics in such large issues as Being—ultimate reality itself—can reasonably expect his deliverances ever to be "proved" or ever to be free of difficult questions.

But was Maslow, with all his talk of knowing reality as it truly is, merely chasing after an empty dream? We cannot answer the question; we simply do not know. Undoubtedly there *is* an "ultimate reality," in some sense or another of the phrase. But whether one comes to know it in those experiences that Maslow called "peak" (or, indeed, whether one can ever come to know it at all) is of course quite another question. Perhaps it is true, as according to Martin Buber the Baal Shem Tov once remarked, that "the ultimate apprehension of knowing is that we cannot know." Even so, we must agree with the rest of what the Baal Shem said—that

> there are two types of not knowing. . . . And the difference between the two —to what can they be compared? To two men who wish to get to know the king. The one enters all the rooms of the king, he rejoices in the king's treasury and halls of splendor, and then he learns that he cannot come to know the king. The other says to himself: Since it is not possible to come to know the king, we shall not enter at all but resign ourselves to not knowing.

And which man is the better for it? That is a question that we must leave the reader to answer for himself.

[19] *Psychology of Being*, p. 88.

5

Value, Religion, and Science

Just finished C. S. Lewis' *The Four Loves,* and
it's still true that I get more out of the theologians than I do out of most psychologists. . . .
Hard struggle to translate it naturalistically,
but when I do it makes sense. . . . Of course,
he winds up with a God—but what of the god
within the person who serves the same function?—A. H. Maslow, Journal entry, 1960.

Value

There is a certain point of view that holds that all statements concerning "value" are really only disguised statements of personal taste and
preference—that they have, in short, the same cognitive status as an approv-
ing (or disapproving) grunt. This point of view is usually spoken of as value
relativism; its most general tenet is that beauty, goodness, and so forth exist
entirely in the eye of the beholder and not at all in the object beheld. Maslow,
of course, held quite the contrary view: he contended that there are at least
some values (the "B-values") that do exist "out there," in the external world,
independently of human judgment.

The path by which Maslow arrived at his theory of value seems to
have been less direct than, say, the one by which he came to his notions on
self-actualization. Indeed, he started out from the position of the value rela-
tivist. In 1935, for example, he wrote (though never published) a little paper
entitled "Aesthetics and Folkways," in which he propounded the argument

that aesthetic judgments, like moral judgments, are "completely dependent upon the peculiar history of the individual and determined by the culture in which he finds himself." Maslow was at this time still somewhat under the spell of behaviorism, which helps to explain why his concluding remarks in the paper sounded like something that Clark Hull himself might have written:

> It seems to me . . . that there is no qualitative general difference between learning that beefsteak is good food and should be responded to by appetite secretions and hunger contractions and learning that certain parts of line, form, and color should be responded to in an aesthetic fashion. Just as beefsteak is nauseating to certain African savages, so will also our art leave them cold and, conversely, there is no difference between a savage learning that decayed shark is good food and that certain sounds are beautiful music.

Beefsteak and decayed shark were of course not among the B-values that Maslow was later to speak of, but it was clear in the paper that he intended his remarks to apply to all such "judgments" of value, however lowly or lofty we might imagine them to be. The view was entirely consistent with his earlier notion that human values are of no consequence at all to the "universe at large."

As best as we can reconstruct it, Maslow's subsequent thinking on the question of values took the following course: first came his discovery (if you will) that self-actualizing persons see the world more clearly precisely because they do not project human values on it; next came his observation that the perceptions of self-actualizing persons are nonetheless infused with a strong, indeed unarguable, sense of value; finally came the conclusion that, if these self-actualizing persons are seeing the world as it truly is (as they must be if their perceptions are undistorted by deficiency-motivation), then the values that they "perceive" must really exist out there in the real world of Being-in-itself.

It was doubtless as a result of this sequence that Maslow's vision of Being-in-itself underwent a certain metamorphosis between, say, the late 1920s and the late 1950s. In his earlier years he held that the universe at large is not the least bit responsive to human values, that it is indeed altogether impersonally indifferent to man as to everything else. He of course continued in this conviction throughout (to do otherwise is to flirt with theism), but not without augmenting it somewhat. Thus in his later years he held that, even though the values of mankind find no reflection in Being, the values of Being do find reflection in mankind—at least, in the best and most exemplary instances of mankind, the self-actualizers. It is not that the self-actualizing person *adopts* the B-values that he perceives; it is rather that he discovers them within himself at the same time that he finds them without. He is, after all, a part of Being himself; thus the B-values are as genuinely existent in him as in any other part of Being—if only he can tear away the veil of deficiency-motivation in order to see them! This is what Maslow spoke of under the heading "dynamic parallelism or isomorphism between the inner and the outer."[1] It is as a result of this isomorphism that many of the B-values turn out to have a happy correspondence with the "best" of traditional human values: beauty, truth, justice, and the like.

Maslow's first published attempt to deal at length with the question of values was a paper written in the late 1950s under the title "Psychological Data and Human Values."[2] He began by referring to the "hundreds of experiments . . . that demonstrate a universal inborn ability in all sorts of animals to select a beneficial diet if enough alternatives are presented from among which they are permitted free choice." He was especially impressed with a piece of research that he had apparently known of since it was first published in 1935.[3] "Chickens allowed to choose their own diet," Maslow observed,

> vary widely in their ability to choose what is good for them. The good choosers become stronger, larger, more dominant than the poor choosers, which means that they get the best of everything. If then the diet chosen by the good choosers is forced upon the poor choosers, it is found that *they* now get stronger, bigger, healthier, and more dominant. . . . That is, good choosers can choose better than bad choosers what is better for the bad choosers themselves.[4]

He went on to suggest that findings of this sort are heavy with implications, since there is what seems to be a parallel phenomenon at the human level. The allusion, of course, was to self-actualization. Whatever else they might be, self-actualizing persons are at the very least good choosers—as evidenced by the success and efficiency with which they have brought their own lives to fulfillment. Might it not be, then, that these manifestly good choosers can (as do the good choosers among the chickens) "choose better than bad choosers what is better for the bad choosers themselves"? For Maslow the answer was decidedly yes: "It is the free choices of such self-actualizing people," he wrote, "that I claim can be descriptively studied as a naturalistic value system with which the hopes of the observer absolutely have nothing to do; i.e., it is 'scientific.' "[5]

This, then, was the basis on which Maslow hoped "to construct a naturalistic, psychological value system . . . derived from man's own nature, without . . . recourse to authority outside the human being himself." He was very eager to stress that the value system so derived would be "scientific" also

---

[1] A. H. Maslow, *Toward a Psychology of Being* (New York: Van Nostrand, 1962), p. 89.

[2] A. H. Maslow, "Psychological Data and Human Values." In *New Knowledge in Human Values* (New York: Harper & Brothers, 1959).

[3] W. F. Dove, "A Study of Individuality in the Nutritive Instincts." *American Naturalist*, 1935, **69**, 469–544.

[4] *Psychology of Being*, p. 143.

[5] *Psychology of Being*, p. 149.

in the sense of being descriptive rather than prescriptive. Thus on several occasions he made such remarks as the following:

> I do not say, "He *ought* to choose this or that," but only, "Healthy people, permitted to choose freely, are *observed* to do this or that." This is like asking, "What *are* the values of the best human beings?" rather than, ... "What *ought* they be?"[6]

The claim, however, must be examined very carefully. It is doubtless true that such a value system would be merely descriptive as far as the "best human beings" are concerned; for it is from them, after all, that it has been derived. But what of ordinary human beings who happen not to be the "best"? Certainly it is not descriptive of their choices; insofar as it applies to them at all, it applies only *pre*scriptively. This is not to say that Maslow wished ordinary mankind to be converted to the values of the self-actualizing person at the point of a sword. Nonetheless, he meant these values to be taken as a prescription in much the same way that a physician means his medications to be taken as a prescription. "I propose," he wrote,

> that we explore the consequences of observing whatever our best specimens [of mankind] choose, and then assuming that these are the highest values for all mankind. That is, let us see what happens when we playfully treat [self-actualizing persons] as biological assays, more sensitive versions of ourselves, more quickly conscious of what is good for us than we are ourselves. This is an assumption that, given time enough, we would eventually choose what they choose quickly. Or that we would sooner or later see the wisdom of their choices, and then make the same choices.[7]

Of course, one may refuse the healing ministrations of the physician, but not without a certain risk. In the present case the risk is that of remaining unself-actualized.

Such were the foundations of that "true science of values, and consequently of ethics" for which Maslow had expressed his hopes a decade earlier in the self-actualization paper. It now remained to inform religion, the traditional custodian of such matters, that it was out of a job.

Religion

We observed in the first chapter that Maslow, from early on, had a quarrel with religion. By now it should be clear that the altercation was actually something of a lovers' quarrel. Certainly there was something about

---

[6] *Psychology of Being,* p. 149.
[7] *Psychology of Being,* p. 159.

religion that Maslow despised; but there was something that strongly attracted him, too. What he found repellent in religion is easy enough to discern: it is what he often spoke of under the headings "superstition" and "supernaturalism." Of course, these epithets could be used to describe everything from knocking on wood to the burning bush on Sinai, and Maslow did in fact so use them. Chiefly, though, his disaffection for religion centered on theism, the belief in "a God or gods," a "Big Daddy in the sky." As an undergraduate he had written:

> Any external agency such as God or [the] Absolute can be tossed off without consideration as improbabilities. For me, a historical account of the evolution of the idea of God is enough to show that I ought not to take it seriously as a cosmological explanation.[8]

In all the years that followed he never wavered in this conviction that theism is a benighted falsehood; neither was he one to suffer falsehood gladly.

We have said that Maslow also found something in religion that attracted him. It would have been better to say that he found something there that, scrubbed clean of its theistic tarnish, might be worth salvaging. His attitude was well expressed in the Preface of his little book of 1964, *Religions, Values, and Peak-Experiences:* "It begins to be clear to me," he wrote, "that in throwing out *all* of religion and everything to do with it, the atheists have thrown out too much." Later in the book he elaborated:

> What the more sophisticated scientist is now in the process of learning is that though he must disagree with most of the answers to the religious questions which have been given by organized religion, it is increasingly clear that the religious questions themselves—[the] religious quests, the religious yearnings, the religious needs themselves—are perfectly respectable scientifically, that they are rooted deep in human nature, that they can be studied, described, and examined in a scientific way.[9]

When seen in this light, the parts of religion that Maslow thought to be worth salvaging should stand out fairly clearly. First, of course, there was the part that answered to his lifelong "Jewish passion" for ethics and utopianism. Then, too, there was the part that comported with his long-standing passion for gnostic revelation, for a glimpse of reality as it truly is, behind the veil of everyday appearances. Finally and most importantly, there was that part of religion that shared his passionate interest in what can only be described as salvation. Surely it requires no great leap of the imagination to see the parallel between Maslow's "self-actualization" and the concept of salvation as it appears in, say, Christianity. Whatever else they may be, self-actualizing

---

[8]Undergraduate philosophy paper, 1929–1930.
[9]A. H. Maslow, *Religions, Values, and Peak-Experiences* (Ohio State University Press, 1964), p. 18.

persons are those who have been saved—if not by the grace of God, then at least by their own efforts and the grace of nature—from the damnation of being mere average human beings, which is to say psychological cripples and hunchbacks. The parallel between the self-actualizing person and the Chassidic vision of the Tzaddik—the righteous, perfected man—is also not difficult to see.

Basic to Maslow's understanding of religion was the idea that "the very beginning, the intrinsic core, the essence, the universal nucleus of every known high religion . . . has been the private, lonely, personal illumination, revelation, or ecstasy of some acutely sensitive prophet or seer." Thus did all religions begin, he thought, and thus too did they all begin with approximately the same content, the same message about the nature of reality. It is, however, "very likely, indeed almost certain, that these older reports, phrased in terms of supernatural revelation, were, in fact, perfectly natural, human peak-experiences of the kind that can easily be examined today, which, however, were phrased in terms of whatever conceptual, cultural, and linguistic framework the particular seer had available in his time." It is also the case that these initial revelations became, in the course of time, institutionalized, codified, and therefore even further corrupted (that is, supernaturalized).[10]

We must, of course, reject religion's supernaturalism, but not at the cost of throwing out the baby with the bath. If we take these "core-religious" experiences and strip them clean of all their supernaturalist accretions, "peel away all the localisms, all the accidents of particular languages or particular philosophies, all the ethnocentric phrasings," we shall find that something very valuable yet remains—namely, the cognition of the B-values. Indeed, we may take it as certain that all of the core-religious experiences amounted (and continue to amount) to precisely this: a revelation of the values inherent in Being itself. Traditional religion has almost always distorted the revelation by insisting that the B-values require a supernatural sanction in order to be genuine. Now, however, we know that these "highest spiritual values . . . have naturalistic sanctions and that supernatural sanctions . . . are, therefore, not necessary."[11]

Maslow went on from here to ask the obvious question: why, then, "were supernatural sanctions for goodness, altruism, virtue, and love necessary in the first place?" Doubtless the question has many answers, but one thing at least seemed "crystal-clear":

> Any doctrine of the innate depravity of man or any maligning of his animal nature very easily leads to some extra-human interpretation of goodness,

[10] *Religions, Values, and Peak-Experiences*, pp. 19–20.
[11] *Religions, Values, and Peak-Experiences*, p. 36.

saintliness, virtue, sacrifice, altruism, etc. If they can't be explained from within human nature . . . then they must be explained from outside of human nature. The worse man is, . . . the more necessary becomes a god. It can also be understood more clearly now that one source of the decay of belief in supernatural sanctions has been increasing faith in the higher possibilities of human nature (on the basis of new knowledge).[12]

It surely goes without saying that by "new knowledge" Maslow meant, "for instance, my studies of 'self-actualizing people' [which] make it clear that . . . there is no need to add a non-natural determinant to account for saintliness, heroism, altruism, transcendence, creativeness, etc." In any event, he argued, we now know that human nature is intrinsically good and, thus, that the goodness of individual human beings does not require the assistance (or goading) of any external agency.

　　Maslow was apparently never disposed to become embroiled in such questions (dear to theistic hearts) as: what, then, is responsible for this intrinsic goodness of human nature? If he had been, he would doubtless have answered: the intrinsic goodness of Being. And here we come to an issue that bears looking into. We suggested earlier that Maslow's "self-actualization" runs parallel to certain religious notions of "salvation." Let us now venture to suggest that his vision of "Being" runs parallel to certain religious notions of "God." Both notions, "Being" and "God," have at least this much in common: they refer to the ultimate reality that lies hidden behind the veil of everyday appearances—self-created, self-sustaining, the ground of all existence and the source of all goodness. Where they differ, of course, is here: the God of the supernaturalists is ordinarily conceived of as a *person,* whereas Maslow went well out of his way to insist that Being is "just impersonally what it is." And yet even here the difference seems to be more of degree than of kind, for it is difficult to see how Being could contain "its values rather than our own" unless it were capable of *valuing,* which is to say unless it had at least this one attribute of a "person."

　　At any rate, although Maslow's Being is clearly not the same as the all-too-personal God of Abraham, Isaac, and Jacob, it does bear a remarkable resemblance to the impersonal "God of the philosophers"—especially to the God of Spinoza, whom, incidentally, Maslow very much admired. He apparently recognized the similarity, for at one point he observed:

The word "god" is being defined by many theologians today in such a way as to exclude the conception of a person. . . . If God gets to be defined as "Being itself," or as "the integrating principle of the universe," or as "the

[12] *Religions, Values, and Peak-Experiences,* p. 37.

whole of everything," or as "the meaningfulness of the cosmos," or in some
other non-personal way, then what will atheists be fighting against?[13]

The answer is that atheists will have nothing at all to fight against, providing
they recognize that all those things to which the word "God" haltingly refers
—mystery, awe, reverence, sacredness, beauty, goodness, and the like—really
do exist!

We saw that Maslow, as an undergraduate, had believed that "any
external agency such as God or [the] Absolute can be tossed off without
consideration as improbabilities." He of course never changed his mind about
"God," but he did seem to relent in his opposition to the "Absolute" (that
is, "Being itself"). Does this mean that he also relented in his opposition to
"supernaturalism"? In his own eyes, certainly not. There are those, perhaps,
who would see his "Being itself" to be every bit as "supernatural" as the
"God" of the theologians. For Maslow, however, it was the most natural of
all natural things. Granted, it transcends the world that we ordinarily experience. That, however, does not mean that the Being revealed through the
core-religious peak-experience is supernatural. It is only that the world of our
ordinary experience is *sub*natural, just as the nonpeak-experience and the
nonself-actualizing person are subnatural.

In any event, religion, properly conceived, is far too important a thing
to be left exclusively in the hands of the religionists. We now know that its
ultimate source, the core-religious peak-experience, "lies well within the
realm of nature"; accordingly, we shall do well to turn it over to that enter-
prise that is best equipped to deal with nature: science. Even now we are
finding that "what the mystics have said to be essential to the *individual's*
religion is . . . receiving empirical support and no longer need rest only on
tradition, blind faith, temporal power, exhortation, etc."[14] How much more
empirical support it might receive, and how much less it might have to rest
on tradition, blind faith, and the like, if only this development were allowed
to continue—if only religion were to be entrusted to science entirely!

But this, alas, requires more than the informed consent of "the more
perceptively religious man"; it cannot fully happen until there is a transfor-
mation within science itself. It should be clear that Maslow was not recom-
mending a mere unilateral "secularizing of all religion"; he was also proposing
a "religionizing of all that is secular."[15] Indeed, he seemed to hold the view
that religion and science at their very best are really quite the same thing—
the endeavor to know (through B-cognition) and to live in accord with

[13]*Religions, Values, and Peak-Experiences,* p. 45.
[14]*Religions, Values, and Peak-Experiences,* p. xiii.
[15]*Religions, Values, and Peak-Experiences,* p. xiii.

(through self-actualization) reality as it really is. He plainly saw, however, that, just as religion is not presently at its best, neither is science.

Science

Maslow had been a critic of "official" science since the early 1940s.[16] His criticism began, in fact, at about the same time that he first hit upon the concept of self-actualization, and we may be sure that the timing was no mere coincidence. If we were to examine his criticisms one by one, we would see that they run almost exactly parallel to the matters he discussed under the headings of self-actualization and B-cognition. By the time his book *The Psychology of Science: A Reconnaissance*[17] appeared in 1966, the connection was perfectly clear.

The first two-thirds of the science book served as a kind of prologue for the main argument, which appeared only toward the end. It was a fairly direct continuation of the points that had been taken up in the religion book two years earlier. "Both orthodox science and orthodox religion," he wrote, "have been institutionalized and frozen into a mutually excluding dichotomy, ... as if a line had been drawn between them in the way that Spain and Portugal once divided the new world between them by drawing a geographical line." Thus everything that is dear to religion is anathema to science, and vice versa; "every question, every answer, every method, every jurisdiction, every task has been assigned to either one or the other, with practically no overlaps." The unhappy consequence is that, just as one must surrender something very important (his intellectual integrity) to become an orthodox religionist, so too must the person who becomes a scientist "automatically give up a great deal of life, especially its richest portions." He is like a monk who can enter the monastery only after making vows of renunciation, and he does so for no better reason than that orthodox science has declared so very much of the "real human world" to be off limits, outside the pale of respectability, *verboten!* As a result, orthodox science is but a "crippled half-science," just as orthodox religion is but a "crippled half-religion."[18]

This self-inflicted crippledness is most apparent to the layman in the short shrift that science gives to values and emotions. Thus, on the one hand,

[16]See A. H. Maslow, "Experimentalizing the Clinical Method." *Journal of Clinical Psychology,* 1945, **1,** 241–243; "Problem-Centering vs. Means-Centering in Science." *Philosophy of Science,* 1946, **13,** 326–331; "Cognition of the Particular and the Generic." *Psychological Review,* 1948, **55,** 22–40.

[17]A. H. Maslow, *The Psychology of Science: A Reconnaissance* (New York: Harper & Row, 1966).

[18]*Psychology of Science,* p. 119.

science proudly proclaims itself to be value-free, "as having nothing to say about the ends, the goals, the purposes . . . of life." Indeed, it goes further and declares that there simply are no such purposes—that the world itself is value-free. Of course, even the scientist may have his personal tastes and preferences; he may prefer Gandhi to Hitler, Bach to rock, leeks to onions, and so forth. But he must never forget that all such "values" are mere subjective evaluations that find no reflection in the world of objective fact. The same is true of his emotions: he must remain ever mindful that they are mere lapses into subjectivity. The scientist perhaps cannot avoid having emotions, but he must not trust them, for they do nothing but distort, distract, and impede.

Small wonder, then, that the scientist is sometimes seen by the layman as "a sort of respectable monster." Small wonder, too, that the more sensitive nonscientists sometimes see science as "a threat to everything that they hold marvelous and sacred, to everything beautiful, sublime, valuable, and awe-inspiring . . . as a contaminator, a spoiler, a reducer, that makes life bleak and mechanical, robs it of color and joy, and imposes on it a spurious certainty."[19] Granted, the layman's impression is often seasoned with a measure of ignorance and misunderstanding. Still, the basic point is a valid one: science does tend to discredit all those things that the more sensitive nonscientist holds sacred.

The plain truth of the matter is that science, at the hands of institutionalized orthodoxy, has been systematically and punctiliously "desacralized." It has been "used as a tool in the service of a distorted, narrowed, humorless, de-eroticized, de-emotionalized, . . . and desanctified *Weltanschauung*." More to the point, it has been used "as a defense against being flooded by emotion, especially the emotions of humility, reverence, mystery, wonder, and awe."[20] The result has been "the banishment of all the experiences of transcendence from the realm of the respectably known and the respectably knowable, and the denial of a systematic place in science for awe, wonder, mystery, ecstasy, beauty, and peak-experience."[21]

And here is the great irony of nineteenth- and twentieth-century scientific orthodoxy. For in denying reality to these things, science has shut itself off from precisely those aspects of the world that are the most real of all! If only the scientist will open himself up to the world, if only he will look on it through eyes unclouded by preconception, he will see that it abounds in value, mystery, wonder, awe, and even sacredness. This is all perhaps beyond the reach of the ordinary scientist, but fortunately there are scientists who are not ordinary, who are in the establishment but not of it. Thus the

[19] *Psychology of Science*, p. 138.
[20] *Psychology of Science*, p. 139.
[21] *Psychology of Science*, p. 121.

"really good scientist," the "psychologically healthy scientist," often does approach his work in just this way:

> with love, devotion, and self-abnegation, as if he were entering into a holy of holies. His self-forgetfulness can certainly be called a transcendence of the ego. His absolute morality and honesty and total truth can certainly be called a "religious" attitude, and his occasional thrill or peak-experience, the occasional shudder of awe, of humility and smallness before the great mysteries he deals with—all these can be called sacred.[22]

These are the all-too-rare scientists who follow their calling "at its highest level," where it is nothing less than "the organization of, the systematic pursuit of, and the enjoyment of wonder, awe, and mystery." They are the ones for whom the greatest rewards are not fame, research grants, and professorial chairs, but rather "such peak-experiences and B-cognitions as these."[23]

The similarity between this really good scientist and the self-actualizing person hardly needs to be spelled out. Maslow, in fact, did not spell it out in the science book, though anyone familiar with his earlier writings would certainly have seen the implication. After all, the chief job of the scientist is to see reality for what it is, and that is a job that the self-actualizing person performs best of all. Indeed, the self-actualizing person tends to be a scientist (in this sense of the term) even without trying; the nonself-actualizing person tends not to be one no matter how hard he tries. It is not just that the self-actualizing scientist would be a better person; it is that he would be a better scientist. He would get the job done better.

The similarity between science at its highest level and religion at its highest level should also be fairly evident. Actually, Maslow did not elaborate on this similarity in the science book as much as he might have. He did urge that science be "resacralized" and that it seek to "discover the values by which men should live."[24] He also noted that the peak-experiences and B-cognitions of the scientist "can equally be called religious experiences."[25] It was in the earlier religion book, however, that he made the point more explicitly. All the old problems of values, ethics, spirituality, and morals, he wrote, are now being

> taken away from the exclusive jurisdiction of the institutionalized churches and are becoming the "property," so to speak, of a new type of humanistic scientist who is vigorously denying the old claim of the established religions to be the sole arbiters of all questions of faith and morals.[26]

[22] *Psychology of Science*, p. 144.
[23] *Psychology of Science*, p. 151.
[24] *Psychology of Science*, p. 124.
[25] *Psychology of Science*, p. 151.
[26] *Religions, Values, and Peak-Experiences*, p. 12.

Faith and morals? This is a curious phrase to be used by one who took his skepticism and atheism so seriously, so proudly. And yet, on second thought, it is not so curious at all. Maslow remarked on several occasions that, had he been born a hundred years earlier, he would most likely have been a rabbi. I would add: yes, a Chassidic rabbi—who secretly studied Spinoza by night. But of course all "if" statements of this sort are idle speculations, *nu*?

In any event, Maslow's religion and science books were the last major works that he was able to complete before his untimely death in 1970 at the age of sixty-two. It is hard to know just how to end this book on Maslow, for he himself was not given to tying things off into neat packages. The tendency is manifest in almost everything he ever wrote. Most writers conclude their sentences with a period—a "stop." Maslow, on the other hand, tended to end his with an "etc.," or even an "etc., etc."—in any case, with a "keep going!"

Epilogue:

"Wonderful Possibilities, Inscrutable Depths"

At the moment of the mystic experience we see wonderful possibilities and inscrutable depths in mankind. . . . Why not ascribe [the wonder of the experience] to man himself? Instead of deducing from the mystic experience the essential helplessness and smallness of man . . . can we not round out a larger, more wonderful conception of the greatness of the human species and the wonderful vistas of progress just faintly glimpsed against the future?—A. H. Maslow, undergraduate philosophy paper, 1928.

If I had to condense this whole book into a single sentence, I [would say] that it spells out the consequences of the discovery that man has a higher nature and that this is part of his essence—or more simply, that human beings can be wonderful out of their own human and biological nature. We need not take refuge in supernatural gods to explain our saints and sages and heros and statesmen, as if to explain our disbelief that mere unaided human beings could be that good or wise.—A. H. Maslow, fragment of an unfinished book, circa 1970.

These two statements were made more than forty years apart. The first was written by a rather rough-edged undergraduate, the second by one of the most distinguished psychologists of his time. Yet, clearly, they were both written by the same hand, inspired by the same vision, and directed to the same goal. Surely this was one of the most significant characteristics of the whole span of Maslow's intellectual life: a most extraordinary coherence and consistency. One is reminded of the Gestalt psychologists' distinction between "good" configurations and "bad" ones; the former are terse, concise, simple, and regular, whereas the latter are none of these things. In this sense, at the very least, it may be said that Maslow's intellectual life approximated a good Gestalt.

But there is another side to this coherence, one that Maslow himself was not often inclined to recognize. "I must insist," he wrote in the concluding paragraph of one of his last papers, "that [my work] is an empirical exploration and reports what I have *perceived,* rather than anything I have dreamed up." Our own appraisal must be a rather different one, for although Maslow's work certainly was an empirical exploration in some degree, it is difficult to see it as that and nothing more. We have seen throughout that he began his psychological work with a certain vision of human nature and of the universe at large, and that, in many instances, the results of his work ended up confirming and extending that vision. It would be unfair to say that Maslow perceived nothing and dreamed up everything; it would be equally unfair to say the opposite. The fairest statement would be that his psychology was a kind of admixture of the two. This, of course, is a characteristic that it shares with every other psychological *theoria,* for they are all admixtures, in varying proportions, of things perceived and things dreamed up.

This last statement becomes less boggling when we recognize that things "dreamed up" (imagined, envisioned) are not necessarily false, just as things "perceived" are not necessarily true. At any rate, the question "Where does it come from?" is only one of the questions that we must ask of a psychological theory. The second is "Is it true?"—or, better said, "Is it headed in the right direction?" If it is, then it is a good theory irrespective of its origins. If it is not, then it is merely another episode in the history of psychology—"of historical interest only," as the saying goes.

But when we put the question to Maslow's psychology, or to any other for that matter, we quickly find that there are as many answers given as there are persons giving them. This is because there are no indisputable, unequivocal "facts" in psychology that oblige us to accept either one view or the other. The most one has to go on is his own global impression of (1) the whole inchoate body of psychological data and (2) the whole of his direct and indirect experience of human nature. All of which is simply to say that any answer must be tentative and humble, since it rests in such large measure on the shifting sands of personal hunch and intuition.

I will not burden the reader with the full weight of my own personal hunches and intuitions. It does seem to me, however, that there is at least one respect—the most important one of all—in which Maslow distinctly *was* heading in the right direction. There is, I believe, a certain face of human nature that has been systematically ignored or denied by all the orthodox psychological "isms." And it is precisely this face that Maslow spent the whole span of his career as a psychologist pursuing, even at the risk of seeming "positively mystic and sentimental." It is the face that is best summed up by his early phrase "wonderful possibilities, inscrutable depths." Of course, it may turn out that these possibilities and depths of human nature are not exactly as Maslow saw them. But that, in the long run, is of little consequence. What matters is that he swam so long and hard against the maincurrent in order to tell us "Yes, they are there—they really do exist!"

Appendix:

Maslow's GHB Notebook[1,2]

May 6, 1945

After fussing along for some years, I have decided to dig into GHB research and do it more formally and rigidly. It's all very difficult though. Lots of problems. As things stand now, I try to be as conscious as possible of insurmountable difficulties, and then I go ahead anyway.

The layout now is to collect students who look like potential GHB and then go through several sieving processes, keeping records all the way. (1) Pick them just by looking at them in class. (2) Then look up their security scores. (3) Then interview them for about an hour. (4) Ask them to write me a memorandum of the interview to the best of their memory for my records. (5) Rorschach test. That's as far as it's gone so far.

Problems. Practically all I've picked show poor Rorschachs. Can't get any satisfaction on this from the experts. What's a good Rorschach [test result] anyway? *Must* study Rorschach [test] in future. Don't know enough about it.

High security scores are obtained by people I'm sure are *not* GHB. Smug bitches some of them. They're so sure they're wonderful, they get obnoxious, lazy, unambitious. Some of my most creative and strong and promising people don't get high security scores. Maybe they're more honest? For example, ——: sort of neurotic, anyway conflicted, and still pretty marvelous. Or is this just very high IQ? How about affect-hunger cases? They're really the nicest people there are and still somewhat insecure, anxious, even neurotic.

[1]See Chapter 3.
[2]Published here by permission of Mrs. Bertha G. Maslow and the International Study Project, Inc.

Selection problems. How come I pick so many more girls than boys? And how come they're practically all very pretty? Is the real basis type? ——for example. Also I'm sure she hates me. Could this have something to do with it?

All in all it seems to work far better with adults. But where to get them?

It would seem that ultimately a full psychoanalysis is the only valid technique for picking. And then, since everyone would show up with some neurotic trends, what degree is necessary for inclusion as GHB?

Also, how about picking apart various qualities I have lumped together? The very sweet and kind, the strong, the creative, the clear-in-mind-about-goals-and-life-in-general? How about somebody like Bertha? Rod Menzies? ——? Not really "adjusted" but very fine and remarkable people anyway.

Another thought. The whole concept has to be defined operationally anyhow. Otherwise I find myself looking for some essence or Platonic idea which may not exist anywhere but in my own mind. Perhaps a whole series of operational researches. Good adjustment according to Rorschach test (like Ruth Munroe's, grade A), according to psychiatric interviews, according to psychoanalysis, according to TAT, according to degree of satisfaction of basic needs, according to degree and quality of achievement. All of these groups would simultaneously overlap to some extent and *not* overlap to some extent. Maybe study at *that* point could really get someplace.

Maybe anyway we'll have to speak of different types of GHB rather than just one type. Maybe they won't be similar in many respects. Maybe they will.

Question: who should do the picking? The picker's values will certainly get in the way. Ought he to be GHB himself? A study of the different people whom different investigators would pick might tell more about the choosers than the chosen.

Anyway there can be at least a minimum requirement. No neurosis, psychosis, psychopathic personality, or obviously psychosomatic diseases. While this will exclude *some* very fine people, it should let most of them through. While it should let through some stinkers, it should exclude most of them.

Also, maybe should use as criterion followups after a certain number of years. Seeing them under *various* circumstances would help, maybe even be necessary. Is it *possible* in our culture for a twenty-year-old to be GHB? With only superficial techniques at my disposal, how can I talk about character structure—the presumably unchangeable part of the person? Maybe they should be married and bear babies before I can judge.

Actually what I've been doing is studying self-actualized adults over fifty or sixty and then getting a list of their common characteristics and then picking youngsters who seemed to me to look like them and show in some degree these same characteristics. But such youngsters might be standing on their ears at age of twenty. Maybe *just* because they're essentially fine people in a cockeyed world?

May 14, 1945

Have completed very interesting research on 4 classes. It's somewhat vitiated because I spoke of some students publicly, but not enough to damage the results. Students in general voted for those I had selected. Also, those I selected had somewhat higher security scores. Those whom the students selected had *much* higher security scores. Apparently they picked for security. But I see quite clearly now that security and GHB are different. High security scorers seem to be sometimes quite smug, self-content, cocky in an unpleasant way. One of them (——) flirted with me in a way that was very annoying. She was *so* certain she was wonderful, that she could easily conquer me or anyone else. And my impression is she was thinking of her grade.

Another one (——) is a damned nuisance in class, always babbling, interrupting, very bad manners, but I can't get her to shut up, no matter how I stare at her meaningfully. She's irrepressible and *quite* unself-conscious. But GHB? No. Another one (——) seems certainly to be quite decent, but in a bourgeois way.

——, whom I picked last semester as very secure, turned out to be security = -80. But now she is married, looks very happy, and reports herself very well adjusted. I would put her down now as a possible nominee.

——, an auditor in Psych. 21R, who attracted my attention as possible GHB, turns out to be definitely not so. Hostile, suspicious, secretive.

Then so many that I pick as GHB have average or fairly low security scores. And still this doesn't make me change my mind about their futures. Again I get the impression that the security test taps only superficial consciousness which is sometimes contradicted by deeper more unconscious security feelings. If we define security as love for others, then it's possible to have such a difference between conscious and unconscious feelings.

—— is the one who *looks* well adjusted, reports herself to be, and whom I still mistrust. I don't know. She is the "communist-personality-type" whom I always mistrust. They seem so hard, so subtly contemptuous. I don't see any love or softness or tenderness or humility in them.

May 24, 1945

Notes from class questions. I pointed to identification with the goals and values of the culture as a mark of health. But this is a mistake unless the culture is worthy of being identified with. Health might mean rejection of these values.

The question comes up of the value scheme behind therapy. Is not the cure of an individual person's bitterness a loss for society because that's one less rebel? Might it not be better for society (although worse for individual) if he remained "sick"? My answer was: is actual social gain more likely to come from health or from bitterness? And if social gain can come from either, how about the *quality* of the social gain? Might it not be worse than what went before? Also, in the U.S., there is too much national wealth for misery ever to become so extreme as to force revolution a la Marx. U.S. improvers have been mostly "good" and healthy people, not bitter or miserable neurotics.

Also, our ruling class has its rule taken away from it when it gets *too* arrogant. It must always compromise and improve or it is no longer the ruling class. Cf. Washington, Jefferson, Lincoln, Wilson, Roosevelt, Jackson, Wallace, etc.

The question of cultural relativity, absolute values, came up often.

I set as the final exam question: "Discuss the various concepts proposed of the desirable personality and present your own views and what you can do to bring it about for yourself." (1) Lectures on self-actualized people; (2) on "fine development" among twenty-year-old students = potentially self-actualizing people; (3) secure people; (4) lecture on normal personality, which should be called "very healthy personality"; (5) Alfred Adler's notions; (6) the average person; (7) the person well adjusted to U.S. culture; (8) the cultural ideals; (9) the religious ideals, e.g., Christ.

June 24, 1945

Summing up, most of the students I picked turned out to have shortcomings. —— was a definite mistake, worst one. Quite hostile and suspicious. —— quite tense, scared, timid—*not* GHB on first interview. Also bad interview with ——, who showed weakness, self-mistrust, etc., to some slight degree. Nice kid, but not GHB. Maybe in future she will be. Also, interview with —— impressed me less rather than more. Interviews with ——, etc., all impressed me upward, more rather than less. Also ——, etc. Doubtful about ——, although not much. Picked ——, just because I disliked her and felt she was *not* GHB even though "well adjusted." She turns out to be one of those excessively high-dominance women, aggressive, rejecting female role, with almost unqualified self-esteem. Hard, cold, demanding, contemptuous. I was right in my first impression.

August 28, 1945

My impression is that there are many more GHBs at Brooklyn College than in my classes at University of Wisconsin. More among Jews, Negroes, foreigners, etc., than among the average white Protestant American.

See *Life* profile on Bing Crosby. Don't know whether it or other biographical material is accurate, so avoid the question of validity by talking about, e.g., "Crosby life profile" rather than the "real" Crosby. Use this same designation with other public figures suggested by Gabriel Almond in his study of liberal businessmen: Andrew Carnegie, Abraham Hewitt, Peter Cooper, Charles Wilson of General Electric Co., Marshall Field III.

I think maybe the early Unitarians, Parker, Channing, Hamel Martineau.

Stroup suggests for reading (after I asked him about the "saintly man") stuff by Martin Buber, Max Weber, Joachin Wach (*Sociology of Religion*), and J. Mecklin (*The Passing of the Saint*).

I looked up an article in *Social Science,* 1945, on the 100 Great Men. The technique that he and Cattell used was "space allotted in encyclopedia." Crap!

September 4, 1945

Decided to add —— to list. She didn't used to be. Conflicted about sex, worried about inability to make love and sex decisions. But she's now to be married soon and looks happy and serene.

September 6, 1945

Bertha suggests ——. Maybe also her husband. I think Yes. Bertha also suggests ——, thinks all annoying habits and shortcomings are products of bad social training and awful current situation. I feel I can't use anyone whose current situation is so bad. Can't tell what comes from character weakness and what from reaction to situation. I thought also of Mr. and Mrs. ——.

September 8, 1945

It finally becomes unmistakably clear that my subjects won't cooperate as they have in other studies. I learned long ago that the older GHBs had an awfully strong sense of privacy, as Ruth Benedict tried to explain to me long ago. She as a matter of fact spoke more freely than any of them about personal things. There was no difficulty about impersonal things, and they would go on at length about their ideas or theories. I don't even dare approach Köhler. Same for Wertheimer. Levy hasn't refused but tends to change the subject. With Oberholzer I never had opportunity. They all seemed uneasy when I told them what I thought of them and what I wanted of them.

Now, to a lesser extent, I find the same with my college students, though probably for different reasons. They just seem bored or evasive or merely polite. I think all the talk and probing just bores them. It's a chore. If I get them in a corner they'll kick through. They won't protest *against* it or refuse; they just don't show up or come late or postpone. —— is the only one I've seen often, and she has uniformly come from one to three hours late. Also, —— stood me up twice even though I had helped him a lot. —— promised to call and hasn't. Same for ——. —— flatly refused information that would involve her husband and has ducked me ever since. So far no one has refused to fill out blanks. Apparently they can do this on their own time and so mind it less.

It's got so that I think of all this as a GHB characteristic and suspect anyone who cooperates eagerly.

What's the difference between these and those in dominance-sex research and all the insecure and neurotic people? They cooperated eagerly. Must be because they could get something out of it. And my present GHB subjects don't get anything out of it. It's pure and simple doing me a favor with little or no return to the subject. It's not personal distaste, because they turn to me easily for help and they like to call socially.

October 16, 1945

During past week have interviewed —— and others. Also gave tests to about six current students whom I shall talk with later. —— and others have failed to get in touch with me yet in spite of my calls and their promises.

October 20, 1945

I suppose a necessary control would be to rely not alone on my impressions from appearance—which may let many slip through—but also on selection by class elections, by Bertha's judgments, and by security test scores and other scores which sample everyone in class. I think I must start that this semester.

I must list separately all those students selected from classes last semester and this. All others were chosen unsystematically and can't be described in terms of the sampling by which they were chosen. It was mostly from going back over all my records and picking the ones who seemed to me in retrospect to have been GHB.

October 29, 1945

Saw —— today and experienced my usual disappointment and scaling down of expectations. Their faces look so much more promising than they actually are. They're all well enough adjusted, happy, psychiatrically untroubled, etc., but still they have no flame, spark, plan, excitement, goal dedication, feeling of responsibility. Would it be different for the men? These women would certainly all make good mothers and wives, but they seem to have little desire to be anything else. Maybe this is a *proof* of their soundness —who knows?

November 9, 1945

This week appointments broken twice by ——, once by ——. —— finally sent in two of the Rorschachs she owes me, but still owes me other material. Never heard from —— or —— after mailing them tests to fill out. Not heard yet from ——. —— never looked me up as she promised repeatedly. —— never stood me up but was always at least an hour late. —— has not yet returned the tests she promised me altho she lives next door. Seems like a constant trait for the group.

November 11, 1945

Today I went through my old classbooks collecting dominance and security scores from my GHB subjects. The general finding is that either the security test is no good at correlating with GHB or else the concept of GHB is quite different from the concept of security. Generally I had not picked, either from appearance or after knowing security scores, those who had the highest security scores. Most of my people had *moderately* high security scores, *not* very high ones. There were also a few with security scores *below* the median.

Upon examining all these data, I came to the conclusion that I've been picking "fine" people whom I could respect and in whom I saw some sort of promise. But many high security scorers are just opposite of this—smug, self-satisfied, "lumpish" in the sense of just not doing much or wanting much, almost torpid. Some seem to me to be stolid. I think this semester I'll examine more carefully the high security scores.

Then some people, like ——, are definitely insecure, even neurotic, and still I respect them and expect good developments. She's a fine, sensitive, thoughtful person with some inner life (some of my high security scorers give the impression of not having *any* inner life).

Added some names retrospectively to possibilities list—to keep my eye on in future—as I went thru class book: ——, etc.

As the work goes on, my objectives shrink more and more. Out of all the dozens of subjects, there's only *one* I'm *sure* of and that's ——. Then I think —— and probably also —— would fit my original notions of the GHB if I had enough data for them. All the rest seem just to be "nice kids" and some of them not even that. Maybe also Mrs. —— and —— at most.

November 16, 1945

—— came to visit me today. Claims she never got tests that were sent her. Renewed promises to help.

Picked another girl out of classes. Noticed her slowly and more and more impressed. By appearance possible GHB. Checked and found out she was elected #2 in her class (after ——) in GHB poll.

I'm going to try a few of the very high security scorers—even those who don't look like much to me.

November 20, 1945

—— supposed to call me today. Didn't. Third or fourth date broken without apology or even explanation.

November 25, 1945

—— Rorschach test.

November 27, 1945

Gave tests to —— in Psych. 28B, not on basis of appearance or on basis of election but because of high security score = +200. Looks like nice kid, maybe 8th or 9th or 10th decile of adjustment, but not impressive. Chattery, gay, sociable in rather childish way. Will pick a few others. Also —— in Psych. 21 had security score = +226.

December 17, 1945

I have been thinking for some time that an especially important characteristic of my GHBs is their ability to see reality more clearly. This showed itself in my security studies, especially among the Blackfoot Indians. It showed itself most, or at least first, in the ability to judge character. They could spot a phony a mile away.

Maybe I should have them try to distinguish fine shades of color. Try Seashore's record on tone differences. Maier test of art judgment. Spot phony poems. Tests of reasoning a la Sell's atmosphere effect experiment. Also suggestion experiments with odors, electricity, etc.

December 19, 1945

Wrong about ——. She's OK. Seems all my mistakes have been due to underestimating homely girls and overestimating pretty ones.

December 28, 1945

Notes on conversation with Stroup describing my research. Borrowed various books on theology, saints, etc. Talked of Tillich, Niebuhr, Augustine. Borrowed Cheney and Meihlin. He told me of Boehme. I asked him about concept of original sin. He told me only Catholics and fundamentalists take it seriously as sects. Unitarians broke away on this question. Parker said "Our disagreement is not so much on the nature of God but on the nature of Man." Other Protestant sects are not for or against it—not fashionable to talk about it.

But the next movement among highbrow theologians in line from Augustine, Kierkegaard, Tillich, and Niebuhr came back to this notion in the form of sin or evil inhering in human nature itself—as part of it.

But I objected. I don't see it. Most of what we call evil or nastiness is a *product*—of frustration, crippling, misery, etc. As for children, they are neither good nor evil. We mustn't use adult terms for them, no more than we should for animals. We can't study the problem, then, because it cannot be seen in children and because the sin of adults is mostly not original. This argument is, we cannot prove "original goodness," but also we see no evidence for "original sin."

The big point is that we just can't find in ordinary mankind the answer to the question.

But what if we study *extra*ordinary people? Certainly a visitor from Mars descending upon a colony of birth-injured cripples, dwarfs, hunchbacks, etc., could not deduce what they *should* have been. But then let us study *not* cripples, but the closest approach we can get to whole, healthy men. In them we find qualitative differences, a different system of motivation, emotion, value, thinking, and perceiving. In a certain sense, only the saints *are* mankind. Others are sick, twisted cripples.

Do we find sin and evil in them? I don't think so. We find neutral equipment which under certain circumstances can make trouble, under other circumstances not. Original sin can be attributed to them only by prejudging the case, e.g., by defining pride as sin and then finding the sin. *Ergo* original sin.

January 13, 1946

So uncertain about my choices, and so many of them turn out badly or doubtful, that I've decided to use the Rorschach as screening device. Until now, I've been taking Rorschachs as the dependent variable and using my judgment as the independent variable. But now will have to add Rorschach to the list of independent variables, which also includes (1) my judgment, (2) security test scores, and (3) self-judgment of subjects.

Mostly this is because I hesitate to plunge into the full study of any individual until I'm fairly sure he's well adjusted. Too much investment of time involved. Does no harm anyway to have a finer screen for selection. Will be convincing to more people.

Ruth Munroe has agreed to score each one on the basis of a checklist. Supplies her with a validation for her checklist hypothesis.

Also I've decided, for next semester, to rely on security test scores a little more for selection of subjects. I can record my intuitive judgments before I get these scores. I'll keep a running record of students who seem to me to be GHB, but I won't select them for interview until I get security scores too, about middle of semester. Can use first half of semester in catching up with this semester's batch.

Will also have to come face to face with dropping the concept of adjustment. See case of ——: well enough "adjusted" in terms of bourgeois culture, but utterly sick in her soul. "Adjusted" but not "healthy."

The notion I am working toward is of some ideal of human nature, closely approximated in reality by a few "self-actualized" people. Everybody else is sick in greater or lesser degree it is true, but these degrees are much less important than we have thought. The self-actualized person is so different from all others that we need a different theory of motivation, perception, emotion, thinking, values, humor, personality, psychopathology, etc.

We may use these people as synonymous with human nature in general because there seems to be no *intrinsic* reason why everyone shouldn't be this way. Apparently every baby has all possibilities for self-actualization, but most all of them get it knocked out of them.

Also have to start writing eventually about the relation of these people to "mystic experiences." Any naturalistic definition of a mystic would be close to a definition of the self-actualized person. Also the fact is that these people (or most of them) have many so-called mystic experiences only never call them that.

Werner suggested that the perception experiments I had thought of would show differences in favor of GHB because others got more easily frustrated and therefore tense and anxious. But I said that could be precisely the point. It is not that I think the perceptual or cognitive apparatus of the neurotic is bad—it is just tempered, inhibited, shackled, blinded by anxiety, rigidity, conventionalization, egocentricity.

I think of the self-actualizing man not as an ordinary man with something added, but rather as the ordinary man with nothing taken away. The average man is a full human being with dampened and inhibited powers and capacities.

We hooked the whole business up with the series of experiments we had planned last year on "intuition." Werner wants to be able to pick out the physiognomic "type." I want to see if this type coincides with GHB. As soon as I feel healthy enough, we'll start it.

January 15, 1946

Notes on Cheney, *Men Who Have Walked with God.* Contrast be-tween Confucius and Lao-tze: "Both were humane, tolerant, and considerate, and both, in a turbulent and degenerate time, envisioned salvation for man in a return to the conditions of the Golden Age. There the resemblance ended. Confucius saw the Golden Age as a time of good manners and noble actions among men and of a science of etiquette and a just code of law. Lao-tze envisioned instead a time when man lived in communion with the Spirit, in natural innocence; when he was in tune with the harmony of the universe and thus required no instruction to make him act nobly. Confucius looked back only to a period when rulers were benevolent and virtuous and subjects, law-abiding and loyal. Lao-tze looked back to an age before rules were necessary. In short, the one sage was a practical reformer, busying himself with laws, regulations, proprieties, and conventions; the other possessed the Golden Age in his heart."

Observe that the contrast is also between extrovert and introvert, color type and movement type. Maybe even between Yogi and "Yogi-Com-missar." Two or more types of saints at least.

Observe also the fact that these and other saints and sages live in a particularly degenerate time. *Must* they be a reaction?

January 18, 1946

Notes on J. Brooks Atkinson, *Henry Thoreau: The Cosmic Yankee.* In general it is as if Thoreau is *trying* to be a mystic, a self-actualized man, but succeeding more in his writing than in his life. Unmarried, practically no friends, not really liberal, definitely maladjusted in college, quite sour in many of his judgments. Emerson: "Henry is—with difficulty—sweet." Con-sidered a crank and a boor by many of his townsfolk.

Also a Yogi. Supported by his friends mostly. "Sauntering through life" is impossible with wife and children and with ordinary obligations to friends, family, and society. One who does this is likely to be parasitic. Not that he was a primitive. He approved of railroads, commerce, ships. Nonethe-less, "he scorned science, because it ignored the 'higher law' ".

January 19, 1946

Trying to clear up notions of self-actualization. I have the idea of using the concept of "ideal" or even "typical type" of the species. Thoreau points out that the eagle has to do what he does, like any other animal, because he is "eagle-like." No animal is cruel or kind or cowardly, etc. These are all human terms and suggest decision at the voluntary, thoughtful level. But animal behavior is determined almost entirely by instincts, by a fate inherent almost entirely in the simple fact of being a member of one species rather than another. The type "instinct" tells the animal (1) when to feel a craving and under what circumstances, (2) *what* to look for to satisfy the craving, and (3) how to behave while looking for this goal object. Thus it's fair to say that the drive, the motivated behavior, and the goal object are largely or primarily determined by heredity.

But it is still possible to make value judgments upon tigers, ants, or oak trees, and *not* on an anthropocentric basis. It need have nothing to do with human values.

To start with the crudely obvious—a lion with no eyes, a tiger with no claws, a deer that can't run, an oak tree without leaves, etc. All these are "bad" or atypical or abnormal or unsuitable. Better to say "deviant" because that is value*less.* For the same reason, we should not use "average," "nonaverage," "extreme," etc.

Of course the obvious universal criterion here would be "survival" viability, or at least the ability to mate and reproduce. But in the long run, this too would be weak because it invokes some value external to the data, to the species. Furthermore, either deviation or lack of it might have survival value. Thus, all tigers without teeth or claws might be allowed to live by the hunter, while other average or "normal" tigers would die. Or, in time of depression, feebleminded children might live better than the average (unemployed) man.

Even so, such biological criteria would still be better than what is available now, by way of countering complete relativity.

But what I think I can really stand on is the notion taken from the biological taxonomists of the "type specimen." This is supposed to be perfect in its own kind, to be standard and typical. And therefore it can be used as an absolute or fixed or constant or invariant (something like the standard foot, pound, quart, etc., of the Bureau of Standards). In other words, this is something like the dictionary, for it is a set of *definitions.* And just as we look up standard usage in the dictionary (it now serves as a fixed criterion even though *originally* it was simply an *ex post facto* reporting of how actual people spoke), so the biologists can compare a doubtful case with the type specimen (the latter is the fixed constant) and so can the behavior or form of an animal be compared with the "type-specimen" which all people have in their minds. What defines the type-tiger? A long list of qualities which, taken together, define the concept. And in this list, most important would be the most unique, the most tiger-ish, *just* those characteristics which *most* differentiate the species from all others. The less important would be those characteristics shared with other species, other families, other phyla, or other animals-in-general.

The type-specimen is the most perfect-in-its-own-kind rather than the most average. It would be the one who had most developed or actualized the unique potentialities of the species—the *finest* specimen of its type.

What does this mean for human beings? That a neurotic is less "good" because he isn't human enough? Because he falls short of the type-specimen? Because he doesn't fit the definition of the species "human being" (like an imperfectly pronounced word, an ungrammatical sentence)?

In any case we can be sure that defining the human species would be a supracultural affair, for it would have to be the *species* that we define.

January 21, 1946

It becomes apparent that I must allow for *various* types of good health, just as there are various syndromes of maladjustment. This is seen especially in my student subjects. There is extroverted and introverted health. There is creativeness, both theoretically minded and practically minded. They are ambitious and contented. Also there are those who seem to me *essentially* and deeply sound, but who are at the moment in trouble. Their symptoms and troubles seem to be superficial, perhaps only situationally produced. There are those with strong sex drive and those without.

I have so many poor Rorschachs among my selectees that it looks as if I can cull only three or four or five clear cases out of my forty or fifty selectees. I won't bother going into extensive interviewing until I am convinced they're OK. So far I feel this certainty only for —— and ——.

Better start reading and abstracting on the concept of adjustment-normality-health.

February 4, 1946

Last Sunday spent day with Mittelmann and Ruth Munroe going over my research and then went through one Rorschach (——). According to Ruth it might be DP, although she couldn't be sure because my inquiry wasn't good enough. Apparently I would have to know more about Rorschach even to administer it well. Spent time since then going through Rapaport and a couple of cases in Beck, Vol. II. Depressed me. Apparently there *is* no well-adjusted person according to the Rorschach. Beck's very best case, the only really "healthy" one in the book, also showed defects that were definite although not serious. Rapaport's normal groups of patrolmen were pretty pathetic. Either Freud was right and everyone is neurotic, or else the Rorschach, while good for psychiatric diagnosis, is no good for normal or healthy people. Or else the people I'm looking for are even rarer than I thought. If I can't trust the Rorschach, then I have no fixed point or independent variable in my research. How can I pick a group of GHBs to experiment on if I have no trustworthy criterion—if the Rorschach shows DP for even my *best* subjects.

On this point I'm reminded of Ann Roe's research on painters whose Rorschachs all turned out to be "uncreative."

Maybe I can get Rorschachs for my older men.

February 9, 1946

Have spent last two weeks studying Rorschach. Feel fairly competent now to judge them. Can easily reject *bad* ones, e.g., ——— and ———. But still have not run across one that looks very good, let alone perfect. But can spot *relatively* good ones, e.g., ———. Of course, must check my impression with those of an expert. Called up Ruth Munroe today—not *one* done yet! Must get someone else.

Can use as a model—almost ideal—the first case in Beck, Vol. II, the scientist-college president.

Anyway, how *could* I expect better from twenty-year-old kids—Jewish ones at that?

Meanwhile I've learned not to trust my security test too far. It's good enough for screening out those who admit themselves to be maladjusted, but those who score high may still not amount to much by the Rorschach test or even by observations. ———, with a security score of over 200, *looked* severely disturbed as well as giving a very bad Rorschach.

Additional men to study: Whitman, Emerson, James, Dewey, Spinoza, Channing, Pascal, Jakob Boehme, Goethe.

February 14, 1946

Pascal is out. Just religious stuff. Read Spinoza by L. Browne. Sounds wonderful.

Conversation with Kepes and Werner. They both agreed that the finest people they have ever met were *not* intellectuals. Kepes spoke of a mason and a peasant woman in Hungary. Werner spoke the same way. But my experience is different. Is the U.S. different from Hungary and Germany in this respect? I recall Wertheimer saying the same thing as Werner. Werner's opinion was that the finest people were so because they were not ambitious. And he considers most intellectuals to be ambitious (necessarily?). Spinoza was unambitious—except maybe for his ideas?

Still looking for heroes. Read in Spinoza (OK), Walt Whitman (?), Goethe (out), and Beethoven (?). Am going to read in Wm. James. Thoreau looked like a man who had the right goals and ideas to a great extent, but was himself only *trying* to reach them, rather than having already attained them. Whitman looks like a show-off, as much an actor as a great man. Goethe was trivial and silly often. Spinoza is the only one who holds up perfectly before scrutiny.

Today received missing Rorschachs from ——, delayed because of awful trouble she had. I shouldn't have gotten angry with her.

February 20, 1946

Received back first batch of scored Rorschachs. —— is doing them under Ruth's direction. Out of ten, at most four are worth continuing with, and two of *these* are questionable. The Rorschach inkblot test is a hard or at least a too snobbish master.

March 1, 1946

Got six more Rorschachs from ——. Long talk, and she seems interested in making a research out of it. I've made for each subject a characterizing and judging statement about level and type of adjustment. She'll correlate these with Rorschach and other test scores. And also she's going to study their peculiarities as a group in the effort to study me and my bases of choice, i.e., one man's ideas about GHB. How do my choices depend upon me?

Ruth Munroe speaks against my effort to seek absolute standards. "It must be relative to what this culture will use or reject."

March 14, 1946

Reread *Jean Christophe*. Much to think of. Is a character as stormy, twisted, uncontrolled ("abnormal"?) as Jean Christophe to be considered GHB? How about Beethoven, on whom this seems to be modeled? There seem to be no rules, criteria, or frame of reference with which to judge Beethoven.

Read *Life of Michaelangelo,* by Symonds. Seems inconceivable that a man who produced works like his should be so querulous, quarrelsome, conventional, etc. I find it hard to believe. Sometimes I doubt the biography rather than the evidence of the statues and paintings.

May 22, 1946

Stopped work for a while. Interested in other things. Also rather puzzled and discouraged by developments in GHB research. —— gave a group Rorschach test to about one hundred of my students about a week ago. Went off OK.

—— gave the Rorschach to —— and never saw her again. Should call her up.

Dictated self-actualization paper to ——, and *she* hasn't showed up either. Must call her.

Today —— called. She's coming tonight. Voluntary.

Have not interviewed anyone in last few months. Don't see anyone really certain in my classes this semester. However, I have about six or eight prospects.

—— picked three names for me to examine. I spoke with them and dictated my impressions to ——. One was ——. Two others I had overlooked: —— and ——. Impressed with —— but not with ——, who strikes me as just about average. Startling thing is that all three, selected as good by Rorschach, have low-to-middle security scores.

Have decided to continue with at least *some* of the prospects whom I rejected after interview. They will be told they are GHB, well adjusted, etc., and followed up as a control group. This certainly can't do them any harm —only good (by suggestion). I think I'd better be careful about picking *only* those who wouldn't be hurt by being lied to.

May 27, 1946

Today gave —— and —— their Rorschach diagnosis from ——. I read it to them (with slight expansion, explanation of terms, etc.) and then asked them immediately to write down what I had read to the best of their memories, as close to verbatim as possible, and then also what they thought of it, agreement or disagreement, and emotional reactions. Our intention is also to observe and jot down subjects' reactions to being told, right out, the Rorschach diagnosis—a procedure usually regarded as dangerous. —— took it very calmly, or at least poker-faced. ——— was heightened, interested, eager, and quite obviously pleased and flattered, asking questions and getting a little pink-cheeked. ——— also asked questions, but very calmly, sedately and (?) thoughtfully. But what will happen when we tell people *bad* news?

Found out that ——— went through OSS screening and was passed (also ———). Would ——— be a good candidate? By now, perhaps—or soon.

May 28, 1946

Today gave ——— her Rorschach report and got her reactions. She showed none in particular. No anxiety, no special eagerness, said nothing. Just looked interested, calm, etc. But last time I spoke to her, she blushed, got flustered, and looked adolescent.

Interviewed ——— at home for several hours. Very nice, pleasant. Also pretty good looking, tall, well built. Have seen her skin look bad, but not today. Talked at length about her history and her family, large, everybody nice and everybody loves everybody else. Happy childhood. Rather eager to talk and seemed to want to make an impression. And yet was quite honest about shortcomings and weaknesses. My original impression was confirmed on the whole, perhaps modified upward a little, and she's not quite as mature as she looks.

June 21, 1946

———was put down by———and Ruth, after inspection of her Rorschach, as very bad—worst they've ever seen. I couldn't see anything worse than immaturity in my interview with her. Definitely my impressions about people and their Rorschachs don't agree very well. For instance, I'm certain ———doesn't amount to much, and yet the Rorschach picked her out as well adjusted. The ones I have picked were often not supported by the Rorschach, and the ones the Rorschach picked haven't impressed me much. David Levy, when I asked him, said the independent variable *must* be the psychiatric interview, behavior, etc. The Rorschach makes mistakes except in the very best hands, and even then it does. For instance———'s diagnoses were rejected by the Columbia graduate psychiatry group. He said anyway, he wouldn't accept———'s diagnosis. Doesn't consider her good. I suppose he'd be shocked to death at using———'s diagnoses.

Anyway I can't lean on the Rorschach as much as I would have liked to—but it will certainly be OK to pick as cases those who pass *all* criteria, including the Rorschach.

September 5, 1946

Back home from Maine. No new thoughts or developments. ——not available as subject—never got friendly enough. Heard from various subjects. ——got fellowship at University of North Carolina. ——is happy at Wisconsin. Certain that he must be called well adjusted. Must get data on him from others at Wisconsin. ——showed up—seems successful, knows just what she wants. Very little humility. Almost condescending to me. Spoke of "good sexual adjustment" as if she had passed some examination with honors. Not soft, warm, yielding, humble, or passive. Proud, hard, self-contained, sure of herself. Certainly well adjusted, certainly doomed to be "successful" but will anything important (humanistically) come from her? I doubt it. Not unless she has some tragedy first and develops a little pity and feeling of smallness. If her husband or children have any weaknesses, I don't think she'll be very kind.

Notes on Clark W. Heath, *What People Are: A Study of Normal Young Men.* First account of grant study. Whole thing in the hands of doctors.

Men selected on basis of grades and physical health (also absence of any notes re psychological maladjustment on medical card).

" 'Normal' is defined as the *balanced,* harmonious blending of functions that produces good integration. Many kinds of such integrations are reflected in widely divergent types of personality and behavior. The 'normal' individual, therefore, here is regarded as the *balanced* person whose combination of traits of all sorts allows him to function effectively in a variety of ways."

In other words, no definition at all.

September 24, 1946

First day at school picked up girl in office who looked good for research (GHB?),——. Asked her to fill out security test. Confirms her appearance. Looks pretty and plump, the kind who is well loved by parents, relatives, and boys.

December—, 1946

Picked up very few in classes this semester. In one class I selected on appearance——, who turned out to be under therapeutic treatment and considers himself maladjusted. ——'s appearance very good, self-estimate very good, first interview very good.

December 29, 1946

Selected some students on appearance: ——in addition to the ones on previous page. But then her security score is only 106, so I don't think I'll pursue it further. Security score for——= -306 with 7 blanks. Arranged for ——to give the Rorschach to——and——. Thought of——, but not sure until his security score came in = 177; will try him. Maybe also——(= 129). Very sweet face. Also thought of——, but her security score turned out to be = -102.

January 10, 1947

Selected——. With——and——that makes only three out of 180 or so students.

January 14, 1947

Leaving NYC for California. Doubt that I will do any work there other than writing book. Leaving research stuff with——. She doesn't seem to be much interested, but might change.

Got from——her description of——, supposed GHB. Nothing in it to contradict an alternative diagnosis of possible trends in PP.

May 25, 1947

Have done practically no work on this since got here [California]. Interesting discussion with Else Frenkel-Brunswik in which she, very much interested, suggested that GHBs are either still struggling or else have struggled in the past and finally come through. Very good! I would also add those who never struggled. We discussed Tolman as possible GHB. Must get dope on him. Also they suggested, or at least asked about,——. Must ask him.

Have read S. Holbrook, *Lost Men of American History*, and C. A. Madison's *Critics and Crusaders*. Several candidates here, but mostly nuts. Kopotkin, Wendell Phillips, Altgeld, Eugene Debs.

But not John Brown, Thorstein Veblen, Daniel DeLeon, Wm. Lloyd Garrison, Margaret Fuller, Emma Goldman, Randolph Bourne. Also *probably* not John Reed, Lincoln, Steffens, Thoreau.

One characteristic to make much of is lack of cant. Also sense of humor, lack of fanaticism, tolerance of others, or whatever it is [whose absence] makes John Brown, Garrison, et al., so distasteful—or Daniel DeLeon, a typical fanatic who can start crusades, inquisitions, purges, terrors. Like the Catholic or communist. Is it respect for the individual as well as the groups? Is it the realization that the group is from this point of view a group of *individuals?* I always got that chill feeling from communists like ——, ——, ——, or even ——that while they might like me, or even love me, they could still kill me or destroy my reputation with no more than a sigh, if this were "for the good of the party," or even if they thought it *weren't* but had been ordered to anyway. John Brown did *just* that. In this sense none of my group is a fanatic. They are not killers of people for "the good of the people" *or* killers of good people "for the sake of advancing goodness." The others kill the individual for the sake of the rubric, the equation, the formula, the concept. Isn't this the same principle as in race prejudice and other stereotype reactions?

By the way, is this the same as "rigidity of personality" of the kind picked up by the Rorschach, or by the Frenkel-Brunswik, Sanford, Levinson studies? These people get the world all classified and then live in their own stable, unchanging world of rubrics and don't even *see* flux, change, individuals, development.

June 10, 1947

Have dictated a form letter to——, and she's sending them to ——, ——, and other subjects. Must check other addresses. So far, answers from——, ——, and ——.

June 12, 1947

Letter from ——, now Mrs. ——.
How about —— as a subject? Certainly a *normal* man, well adjusted,

does his job well, good husband, good father, loves his dog, always cheerful, crackerjack at his truck driving, trusted by boss, slated for promotion. Was mate on same boat. Got captain's papers. In navy, in school for Quartermaster. Invited over for a Sunday, nothing to talk about. We were bored, but he seemed pleasant, cheerful, and seemed to enjoy the quiet afternoon. Have known him now in weekly or biweekly contacts for four months.

August 20, 1947

Couple of weeks ago in Berkeley discussed GHBs with Lois and Gardner Murphy. Some disagreements on people. They doubted ——on grounds of dominating or, rather, patriarchal relation to his wife. They doubted —— because she is "typical liberal" who is convinced she's right. That didn't sound sensible to me. They questioned —— on grounds they refused to reveal, saying I would find out. They suggested and agreed upon Mr. and Mrs. —— and others.

From what they say, I mistrust their judgment. For instance —— is certainly too tense and apprehensive to be GHB. What they objected to in ——didn't sound sensible. *But* if I don't trust their judgment, this is the same as saying they don't trust mine. What objective fact may be appealed to?

February 1, 1948

Have talked with —— about five hours by now. Absolutely no sign of neurosis that I can see and yet nothing positive either. Bovine happiness and security.

To read paper to Motivation Group at Berkeley (Krech, etc.), stressing difficulties. Think it's about time to publish what I have.

So far —— seems to hold up in spite of criticisms.

January 25, 1949

—— is in the "almost" class. —— is another one. —— is out after talks with McLeod and Krech. A fireman in a restricted cultural tradition.

March —, 1949

On trip saw —— at Cornell. Looks good still. Reacting very nicely to the discovery that she's not very bright. —— is now married. Saw Pop Schrank. Ruth Benedict died.

April —, 1949

Writing up self-actualization stuff again for publication.

September 28, 1949

Back in Brooklyn. —— collecting stuff for family background questionnaire. ——, grad student, to do TATs on GHBs. Doing all telephoning, re-establishing contact for me. Already have seen ——, who is a teacher, soon to be married and very happy (and self-satisfied, even smug). —— called. Can't come because three months pregnant and works all day. Will write. Trying to locate ——. So far one person only has refused cooperation (——, I think) on ground that she has no time. —— to visit next Friday.

Have spent much time organizing my files, rearranging data, getting ready for work. But too busy with college, too tired.

Self-actualization paper all finished and accepted for Wolff's journal. Read by Raab who had fits: "Too fuzzy."

Saw —— in Los Angeles twice. *Very* nice. Making wonderful adjustment for unmarried, friendless woman with no looks and no figure.

Checking over list of possible GHBs. Of these, —— is out. His behavior in Berkeley was so irresponsible as to suggest psychopathic personality. Not sure, but certainly looks like it. His security score in 1941 was 98.

—— improved, went through analysis, but could not possibly be called either healthy or well adjusted as a woman.

Met ——, who's now my neighbor. Has a kid. Looks handsome as ever. She is now Mrs. ——, or something like that. Will try to talk with her.

Heard very bad reports about ——. Said he was a flop in OSS, conceited, disliked, etc. But they themselves have such bad judgment, I reserve decision.

—— in Berkeley. Married. Still more talk than doing. I spoke sharply to him and never saw him again.

—— (Mrs. ——) insane for a time.
Must look up ——.

September 30, 1949

At Brooklyn College picked up —— on grounds of appearance. But minus on self-appraisal, on security test, interview, etc. But will follow because she looks like nice person.

How about ——? Looks like a nice guy.

Saw ——, who came unwillingly to take TAT. Looked bad, shifty-eyed, removed, almost neurotic or insane. After a time she settled down, but certainly no friendliness or contact. I was treated with suspicion. She has been severely ill, was close to death for months. Broke off with boy. Now for year with another, very unsatisfactory.

October 7, 1949

Saw —— (Mrs. ——). She had had a successful psychoanalysis. Spoke for an hour or two. Seemed a little tense to me, didn't look as happy as she said she was. Could be because no children, which she badly wants and husband doesn't.

October 11, 1949

—— came to house. Long talk.

Letter from ——, who is neither happy nor unhappy but "in a vacuum." No job, no interests, no prospects. Prefers not to work with me because she can't see what's in it for her. Since I was glad to get rid of her, I let it go at that and said that if I ever needed her in future I'd call her.

Stuff from ——. Extremely insecure family background, PP father (?). How did she come out so nicely?

December 20, 1949

Finally started selecting subjects from my classes. Of all things, got a big crop from my freshman class and a very small one from my senior and grad classes. Used security test score and appearance as preliminary screening, seeing for interview *everyone* with high security score even if appearance negative. Rejected only a few after interview on ground that, even where I am doubtful, the Rorschach and TAT will give better grounds for dismissal. (Also rejected some on appearance and behavior alone even without interview.)

     —— rated + on appearance in class; also ——, who got a security score = 20 and rated self as mixed up, etc. Others in class with security scores below 10 are —— 6, —— 1, and —— 7. I would have picked one on appearance, but never the other two.

     Saw —— today after her letter in which she mentioned she had had a breakdown. Turned out to be (I think) an acute unexpected schizophrenic episode. She had shock treatments (no psychotherapy) in private hospital plus six or eight months recuperation and is OK since. *Still* doesn't look schizzy. Would like to get married. Works as office secretary. Likes it well enough, but not too much. Prefers to be busy every minute. She *thinks* she had orgasm with men and (I gather) more easily by herself. Spoke very vaguely of sex, refused to give details, hinted at shameful things. Implied not too strongly sexed. . . .

Index